THE COMPLETE
GONE WITH THE WIND
TRIVIA BOOK

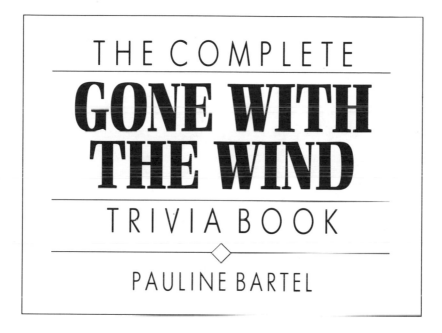

THE COMPLETE
GONE WITH THE WIND
TRIVIA BOOK

PAULINE BARTEL

TAYLOR PUBLISHING COMPANY
Dallas, Texas

◆

FOR GEORGE

Copyright © 1989 by Pauline Bartel

Published by
Taylor Publishing Company
1550 West Mockingbird Lane
Dallas, Texas 75235

Photographs from the Bettman Archive, the Kobal Collection,
Turner Entertainment, and the author's collection.

Designed by Lurelle Cheverie

Composition by High Resolution, Inc.

Library of Congress Cataloging-in-Publication Data

Bartel, Pauline C.
    The complete Gone with the wind trivia book / Pauline Bartel.
        p.   cm.
    Includes Index.
    ISBN 0-87833-619-2 : $9.95
1. Gone with the wind (Motion picture) 2. United States—
History—Civil War, 1861-1865—Motion pictures and the war.
I. Title.
PN1997.G59B37   1989
791.43'72—dc20   89-30442
                                                                CIP

Printed in the United States of America

10 9 8 7 6

Acknowledgments

I would like to thank the following individuals for their unflagging support and encouragement: R. B. Bartel, Terry Brown, Jackie Craven, Diane Daley, Jim Donovan, David Drotar, Nancy Griffis, Shelby Harrison, Joyce Hunt, Kate Kunz, Maureen Lewicki, Peg Lewis, Rebecca McBride, Arnold Madison, Anne Matthews, Carol and Alice Michon, Marie Musgrove, Maggie Oldendorf, Doreen Shea, Mavis Valley, Lynne VanDerhoof, Lynn Wilson; and special thanks and much love to my mom.

Contents

◆

GWTW

Introduction

◆

"There has never been a picture like David O. Selznick's *Gone With The Wind*."

So wrote Kate Cameron, movie critic for the *Daily News*, in her four-star review of the film's premiere in New York City on December 19, 1939. And millions still agree. Today, this Academy Award–winning, box-office champion remains one of the most popular, best-loved movies in history.

Gone With the Wind celebrates its fiftieth anniversary in 1989. In honor of this cinematic milestone, I was inspired to write a book that will surprise and entertain any *GWTW* buff. *The Complete GONE WITH THE WIND Trivia Book* proves that *GWTW* is more than a film: It is a phenomenon. And the wonder of *GWTW* continues to the present day:

• The novel has sold more than 25 million copies in 27 languages and still sells almost 50,000 hard cover and 250,000 paperback copies a year.

• Ticket sales, foreign rights, and rentals and sales of the *GWTW* videocassette have earned more than $840 million.

• In May 1985 when *GWTW* debuted as an $89.95 double videocassette, it marched toward the top of sales charts, claiming second place behind *Star Trek III*.

• In 1986 at the novel's fiftieth anniversary celebration, held in Atlanta, collectors and *GWTW* fans bought 50,000 Margaret Mitchell commemorative postage stamps.

• After years of refusal, Margaret Mitchell's estate has finally authorized a sequel to the novel. A film sequel is likely to follow.

Through *The Complete GONE WITH THE WIND Trivia Book*, you can explore the *GWTW* phenomenon from the writing and publishing of Margaret Mitchell's novel through the Hollywood frenzy of transforming the book into the film. You can guess who spoke quotable quotes from the movie, and you can experience the country's reaction as *GWTW* swept across America.

Do you know the significance of the *GWTW* award for Best Supporting Actress in 1939? Do you know what incident occurred on Academy Award night that was destined to change all future Oscar presentations? Do you know when *GWTW* first appeared on network television? *The Complete GONE WITH THE WIND Trivia Book* answers these questions. The book takes you right up to the present day when the appetites of fans have been whetted by the novel's half-century birthday and the speculation about the continuing story of Scarlett and Rhett in novel and film sequels.

What makes me such a *GWTW* expert? I was blown away by *the Wind* at the age of sixteen when, during Christmas vacation from school, I accompanied my mother to see the film's latest reissue. As we inched along the line at our local theater, I remember catching sight of the film's poster housed in a glass case near the ticket window. I glanced at a provocatively dressed Vivien Leigh in the passionate embrace of an open-shirted Clark Gable.

"Who are they in the movie?" I asked my mother.

"You'll find out," was my mother's cryptic reply.

In the next four hours, find out I did. I was captivated by the dashingly romantic, dark-suited Rhett Butler (wearing a black-and-white cravat) as he watched Scarlett ascend the staircase at Twelve Oaks. I identified with Scarlett's love for Ashley, as only a sixteen-year-old suffering the pangs of unrequited love could. I struggled with Scarlett through the destruction of the Civil War and the devastation of Reconstruction. I put on the green velvet drapery dress and went to Atlanta with Scarlett to try to get tax money from a jailed Rhett. I was with her when she was attacked at Shantytown, when she was caught in Ashley's arms, and when Bonnie was thrown from her pony. By the end of the movie, I had tears streaming down my face (having run out of my meager supply of Kleenex) and was thoroughly in love with this spectacular story of indomitable will and indestructible spirit.

That love affair endures. I've been a "Windie" now for more than twenty years, and I've seen the movie almost as many times. I have an extensive collection of *GWTW* books and memorabilia. As further evidence of my fervor, I am foster mother to a cat named Rhett Butler.

The Complete GONE WITH THE WIND Trivia Book is a true labor of love. It is my fiftieth anniversary tribute to Margaret Mitchell, David O. Selznick, Vivien Leigh, Clark Gable, Olivia de Havilland, Leslie Howard, and the countless others who were responsible for making *Gone With the WIND* "the most magnificent motion picture ever."

Don't "think about it tomorrow"; turn the page today and start exploring *The Complete GONE WITH THE WIND Trivia Book.*

AUTHOR! AUTHOR!

◆

DID YOU KNOW THAT
MARGARET MITCHELL . . .

• was born, raised, and lived her life in Atlanta, Georgia?

• enjoyed listening to Civil War stories told to her by Southern veterans, family, and friends?

• was married twice? She married Berrien "Red" Upshaw in 1922. Her second husband, whom she married in 1925, was John R. Marsh. He had served as best man at her first wedding.

• kept her maiden name after marriage: Margaret Munnerlyn Mitchell?

• published only one magazine piece, "Matrimonial Bonds," which appeared in a local periodical, the *Open Door*, in 1925?

• worked for the *Atlanta Journal Sunday Magazine* as a reporter at a salary of twenty-five dollars a week? Her most famous interview was with Rudolph Valentino.

• resigned in 1926 and filled her time researching information on the "War Between the States"?

• was confined to her apartment by a sprained ankle and began writing a Civil War novel?

• wrote her book using a Remington portable typewriter and yellow copy paper?

• wrote the last chapter of *GWTW* first?

• kept completed chapters of *GWTW* in manila envelopes that she stacked on the floor of her apartment?

- originally called her heroine Pansy O'Hara?
- originally called Tara Fontenoy Hall?
- originally called Melanie Permalia?
- reported to friends that "It stinks" when they asked how her book was going?
- received a $500 advance from Macmillan for the novel?
- used *Another Day* as the working title for her book. Other titles she considered were *Milestones, Jettison, Ba! Ba! Black Sheep, Not in Our Stars,* and *Bugles Sang True?*

- found the actual title for her novel in the first line of the third stanza of Ernest Dowson's poem "Non sum qualis eram bonae sub regno Cynarae" ("I have forgotten much, Cynara! gone with the wind")?
- suffered from eye hemorrhages after constant work preparing the manuscript for publication?
- asked her attorney father, Eugene Mitchell, to review the manuscript for historical accuracy?
- dedicated the book to her husband: "To J.R.M."?
- never wrote another book after *GWTW* was published?

Margaret Mitchell began writing *Gone with the Wind* in 1926 and continued working on it on and off for ten years. Being a private person, Margaret told only a few close friends about her novel. One of those friends, Lois Cole, had become an associate editor at the Macmillan Company and told Macmillan vice president Harold Latham about Margaret's novel.

"No one has read it except her husband," Lois Cole told him, "but if she can write the way she talks, it should be a honey of a book."

In April 1935, Latham launched a three-month literary tour through the United States in search of new authors. His starting point was Georgia. He met Margaret at a luncheon in his honor at the Atlanta Athletic Club. Remembering Lois Cole's recommendation, Latham asked if Margaret would let him read her manuscript. Margaret was flattered but knew the awful shape her manuscript was in. The yellow paper had faded, and there were many changes made in pencil. She had different versions of some chapters, and she hadn't even written an opening chapter. Feeling embarrassed, Margaret denied she had anything to show him.

Latham gave Margaret other opportunities to share her manuscript, at a lunch the following day for local writers and at a tea the day after that. Each time, she refused to discuss her work. She did promise, though,

 A YOUNG MARGARET MITCHELL.

that Latham would be the first to look at her manuscript when she was ready to show it. Margaret, however, thought that this was an unlikely possibility. But something happened after the tea that changed Margaret's mind—and her life—forever.

During the ride home, Margaret and a number of aspiring authors chatted about the evening's events, and someone asked Margaret why she hadn't given her book to Mr. Latham. Margaret admitted that the writing wasn't any good and that she was ashamed of it. One of the writers who was surprised to learn of Margaret's book remarked that she didn't think Margaret took life seriously enough to be a successful novelist. She even found fault with the fact that Margaret's manuscript had never been rejected by a publisher.

"*I've* been refused by the very best publishers. But my book is grand," she told Margaret. "Everybody says it will win the Pulitzer Prize. But, Peggy, I think you are wasting your time trying. You really aren't the type."

At that, Margaret became angry, and she remained angry when she arrived home.

"I was so mad still that I grabbed up what manuscript I could lay hands on," Margaret said, "forgetting entirely that I hadn't included the envelopes that were under the bed or the ones in the pot-and-pan closet, and I posted down to the hotel and caught Latham just as he was about to catch the train. My idea was that at least I could brag that I had been refused by the very best publisher." Margaret gave the large pile of envelopes to Latham and hurried home. Since Latham had no room in his bags, he bought an extra suitcase to carry the manuscript with him.

By the time Margaret cooled down, she realized what she had done. But it was too late. Harold Latham, on a train bound for New Orleans, was thoroughly engrossed in Margaret's manuscript. And the result of Margaret's impulsive act? Three months later, the Macmillan Company offered her a book contract.

PARALLELS BETWEEN SCARLETT O'HARA AND MARGARET MITCHELL

Scarlett O'Hara

1. Married Lieutenant Charles Hamilton, who died of measles complications shortly after the Civil War began.
2. Shocked Atlanta society by dancing with Rhett Butler while in mourning.
3. Experienced the pain and confusion of the populace fleeing Atlanta after the burning of the depot warehouses.

4. Returned to Tara from Atlanta to find her mother, Ellen O'Hara, dead of typhoid. She had worn herself out nursing others.

5. Had three husbands: Charles Hamilton, Frank Kennedy, and Rhett Butler.

Margaret Mitchell

1. Was engaged to Lieutenant Clifford Henry, who was killed on a battlefield in France during World War I.

2. Shocked Atlanta society by performing a French Apache dance at a Junior League ball.

3. Experienced the panic and confusion that took place during the 1917 Atlanta fire.

4. Was called home to Atlanta from Smith College in Northhampton, Massachusetts after her mother was stricken with Spanish influenza. Mrs. Mitchell, weak from nursing others during the epidemic, died before Margaret reached home.

5. Loved three men: Clifford Henry, Berrien "Red" Upshaw, and John Marsh.

GWTW: A NOVEL QUIZ

1. Why did Margaret's character Gerald O'Hara leave Ireland?
2. Gerald was sent to his brothers who were successful Savannah merchants. What were their names?
3. How did Gerald obtain both his valet and his plantation?
4. What was the name of Gerald's valet?
5. Who was raised in the bedroom of Ellen O'Hara's mother?
6. What was Ellen O'Hara's maiden name?
7. With what cousin was Ellen passionately in love?
8. Under what circumstances was he killed?
9. How old was Scarlett when the novel opened?
10. What was Scarlett's first name?
11. What fragrance did Scarlett always associate with her mother?
12. Where did Scarlett receive her education?
13. What were the given names of Scarlett's sisters, Suellen and Carreen?
14. How many brothers did Scarlett have?

15. Who was Suellen's beau?

16. Whom did Carreen love?

17. Why did Gerald O'Hara visit Twelve Oaks the day before the barbecue?

18. Who was the stepdaughter of Gerald's valet?

19. Who were Ashley Wilkes's sisters?

20. Who were the beaux of the Wilkes girls?

21. What was Mrs. Tarleton's first name?

22. What business did Mrs. Tarleton manage?

23. What was the identifying characteristic of Mrs. Tarleton's daughters?

24. Who were the Tarleton sons?

25. Who was the body servant for the Tarleton twins?

26. According to his neighbors, what was Hugh Calvert's big mistake?

27. How did Hugh Calvert's daughter follow in his footsteps?

28. Who were Scarlett's three children?

29. Why had the city of Atlanta always interested Scarlett?

30. What was Aunt Pittypat's real name?

31. Who was Aunt Pittypat's house servant?

32. Who was Aunt Pittypat's brother?

33. How much did Gerald O'Hara lose to Rhett Butler while playing cards?

34. What was Rhett Butler's middle initial?

35. When Ashley was reported missing, who discovered his whereabouts?

36. Where was Ashley held as a prisoner of war?

37. Which member of the Home Guard was Scarlett shocked to see marching to the battle near Kennesaw Mountain?

38. On what date was Melanie's son born?

39. After her return to Tara, Scarlett walked to Twelve Oaks looking for food. What did she eat there?

40. Scarlett rode on horseback to visit the Fontaine family. What was the name of their plantation?

41. When the Yankees returned to Tara, where did Scarlett hide the wallet taken from the deserter she had killed?

42. Which of Tara's rooms did the Yankees set on fire before they left?

43. Who was the one-legged Confederate soldier who stayed to take care of Tara?

44. Whom did he marry?

45. Why was Rhett in jail in Atlanta?

46. Who killed Jonas Wilkerson?

47. What became of Scarlett's youngest sister?

48. Who protected Scarlett on her rounds to the mills?

49. What did Bonnie Butler name her pony?

50. By the end of the novel, how old was Scarlett?

GWTW HITS THE BOOKSTORES

• Macmillan's spring 1936 catalog devoted a full page to announcing GWTW's debut.

• A typographical error escaped the eyes of Macmillan's catalog proofreaders. The catalog's inside front cover referred to the book as *Come with the Wind.*

• Macmillan initially placed a print order for 10,000 copies of GWTW and planned to formally release the novel on May 5, 1936.

• The Book-of-the-Month Club named GWTW its feature selection for July 1936.

• Because of the book-club sale, Macmillan delayed the formal release date for GWTW to June 30, 1936. The publisher still shipped copies of the novel to bookstores in May.

• The prepublication price of GWTW was set at $2.75. But after considering typesetting and printing costs for the 1,037-page novel, Macmillan raised the publication price to $3.00.

• Word-of-mouth news about GWTW accelerated the public's demand for the new book. Macmillan ordered three subsequent printings during the month of June.

• Before the official release date had even arrived, a total of 100,000 copies of GWTW were in print.

• First-edition book collectors were confused! Copies of GWTW purchased at publication bore "Published in June" on the copyright page (there had been three printings in June), yet earlier copies carried "Published in May." Collectors flooded Macmillan with requests for clarification. As a result, Macmillan was compelled to send out form letters explaining that copies of the novel with the May publication date were the real first editions.

• Bookstores were unable to keep *GWTW* on the shelves or in their window displays. Proprietors complained that bookstore windows were broken and that thieves were making off with copies of the novel.

• One month after publication, 201,000 copies of *GWTW* were in print. By September 1936, with 370,000 copies in print, *GWTW* was declared the fastest-selling book in history.

• The one-millionth copy of *GWTW* was printed on December 15, 1936. Macmillan made this most significant volume a gift to Margaret Mitchell.

GWTW: THE CRITICS' CHOICE

"This book has been waiting to be written for many years."
HENRY SEIDEL CANBY, Book-of-the-Month Club

"The story, told with such sincerity and passion illuminated by such understanding, woven of the stuff of history and of disciplined imagination, is endlessly interesting."
HENRY STEELE COMMAGER, *New York Herald-Tribune Books*

"This is beyond doubt one of the most remarkable first novels produced by an American writer. It is also one of the best . . . Although this is not a great novel, not one with any profound reading of life, it is nevertheless a book of uncommon quality, a superb piece of storytelling which nobody who finds pleasure in the art of fiction can afford to neglect . . . In sheer readability, it is surpassed by nothing in American fiction."
J. DONALD ADAMS, *The New York Times Book Review*

" . . . one of the great novels of our time."
The Chicago Daily News

"It will be hailed as The Great American Novel, and it will deserve all the praise that it receives."

The Boston Herald

" . . . more than a novel, perhaps a whole library in itself."

The New Yorker

" . . . this book contains a literary experience rare as a roc's egg: the full realization of characters."

Newsweek

"*Gone with the Wind* is very possibly the greatest American novel."

The Publishers' Weekly

"There ought to be a law that hangs anyone who writes a novel over 350 pages long. But I fell into this one as into a swimming pool. I don't know whether *Gone with the Wind* is a true picture of the South in those days. But I do know it is a true picture of the picture of those days that I got as a child from listening to aging, graying relations and friends of their youth."

MILDRED SEYDELL, *Atlanta Georgian*

"The history of criticism is strewn with the wrecks of commentators who have spoken out too largely, but we are ready to stand or fall by the assertion that this novel has the strongest claim of any novel on the American scene to be bracketed with the work of the great from abroad—Tolstoi, Hardy, Dickens . . . "

EDWIN GRANBERRY, *New York Sun*

" . . . an unforgettable picture . . . a torrent of narrative . . . an extraordinary book."

HARRY HANSEN, *World Telegram*

"It is an overwhelmingly fine novel . . . a broad canvas that throbs with color and life."

CHARLES HANSON TOWNE, *American*

IT'S ONLY A RUMOR

Margaret Mitchell was not your average celebrity. She was a private person who shunned the spotlight, avoided interviews, and steered clear of public appearances. As a result, people who were hungry for information about her willingly believed the most outrageous rumors.

Rumors began flying almost as soon as *GWTW* was published. And there was no stopping them. Some of the more colorful ones claimed that Margaret Mitchell

• was coached in writing *GWTW* by the editors at Macmillan;

• wrote *GWTW* on company time when she was a file clerk for an Atlanta insurance company;

• was turned down by many publishers before Macmillan bought the novel;

• paid Sinclair Lewis to write the book for her;

• talked her brother into writing *GWTW*;

• copied her novel directly from her grandmother's diary;

• sold the novel to Macmillan for a paltry two hundred fifty dollars;

• received so much money from Macmillan that she was able to purchase a large Long Island estate;

• was in hiding on an Alaskan mink farm;

• occupied a suite of rooms at an Atlanta hotel for weeks, during which time she was drunk and threw her money away;

• supplied Macmillan with an additional chapter that revealed whether or not Scarlett got Rhett back. The chapter could be had by sending one dollar to the publisher.

• used a rubber stamp to autograph copies of her book;

• was insane, or dying from leukemia, or going blind, or had a wooden leg;

• would only write by the light of an oil lamp;

• sold articles to women's magazines for millions of dollars;

• refused to come to the breakfast table until her husband had placed two dozen American Beauty roses at her place;

• was in Reno divorcing her husband;

• purchased and restored an antebellum mansion so that Selznick would have a background setting for the film;

• was in charge of selecting the entire cast of *GWTW*;

• was secretly taking acting lessons at Selznick's studio so she could play Scarlett;

• had definitely been selected to play Melanie;

• was behind the camera directing the film;

• received a blank check from Louis B. Mayer to write a sequel to *GWTW*.

Such fanciful tales were the price of fame for Margaret Mitchell. She was amused by some and hurt by others. And as a result she spent a good deal of time trying to debunk the myths by telling people, "It's only a rumor."

AN AWARD-WINNING NOVELIST

Two important awards were bestowed upon Margaret Mitchell in the spring of 1937. The first was the annual award of the American Booksellers Association (now the National Book Awards). The second was the prestigious Pulitzer Prize.

On the recommendation of the Pulitzer School of Journalism's advisory board, the trustees of Columbia University named *Gone with the Wind* "the most distinguished novel of the last year."

Margaret's Pulitzer Prize of a thousand dollars caused a sensation in Atlanta. When the news hit the Associated Press wires, local newspaper reporters sought out the author for a statement. But Margaret Mitchell was unaware that she had won. When the congratulatory telegram arrived from the Columbia Trustees, she was having dinner with visiting Macmillan vice president Harold Latham. Reporters scoured the city for her.

Lamar Q. Ball, city editor of the Atlanta *Constitution*, finally tracked her down by telephone at her father's Peachtree Street home. Not taking any chances with the publicity-shy Mitchell, Ball then hurried from his office with a photographer (even though the paper was on deadline) to the Mitchell residence to cover the story himself.

"I don't know which impressed me most," Margaret later quipped, "winning the Pulitzer Prize or having the city editor of the *Constitution* leave his desk."

In 1938 Margaret's two previous honors were joined by a third. The Southeastern Library Association bestowed upon her the Carl Bohnenberger Memorial Medal. The award was given for "the most outstanding contribution to Southern literature" in the previous two

UPI/BETTMAN ARCHIVE

MRS. MITCHELL READING CONGRATULATIONS
FROM FRIENDS FOLLOWING THE ANNOUNCEMENT THAT
GWTW HAD WON THE PULITZER PRIZE.

years. There was no doubt that Margaret was clearly an award-winning novelist.

GWTW: A GIFT FOR THE FUTURE

On September 23, 1938 a copy of *GWTW* was enclosed in a time capsule and buried in Flushing Meadows, New York at the site designated for the 1939 World's Fair. The capsule, destined to be opened in the year 6939, contained over a hundred other representative items of life in the late 1930s. Among the items were newspapers, magazines, newsreel footage of Franklin D. Roosevelt, the Lord's Prayer written in three hundred languages, an almanac, dictionary, wristwatch, can opener, slide rule, telephone, alarm clock, a woman's hat, and a plastic Mickey Mouse cup.

HOW *GWTW* WAS SOLD TO THE MOVIES

In 1936, Annie Laurie Williams, an agent for Macmillan, sent copies of *GWTW* to movie studios that might be interested in obtaining film rights. Katherine "Kay" Brown, story editor for the New York office of Selznick International, read the book and could barely contain her excitement. She immediately wired her boss, David O. Selznick, and begged him to read the long synopsis of *GWTW* she was sending to him.

Selznick read the synopsis and winced. Another Civil War story! Selznick knew that, with the exception of D.W. Griffith's 1915 film *The Birth of a Nation*, movies about the Civil War were bad news at the box office. Paramount's *So Red the Rose* had proved that just the year before with its dismal ticket sales. Selznick also had no major actress under contract who could undertake the lead. So reluctantly, Selznick wired Kay Brown, "Most sorry to have to say no in face of your enthusiasm for this story."

But then Selznick rethought his decision and sent a follow-up wire to Kay Brown: "I have thought further about 'Gone With the Wind' and the more I think about it, the more I feel there is [an] excellent picture in it." Selznick suggested that Kay bring *GWTW* to the attention of the executives of Pioneer Pictures, the Technicolor division of Selznick International. Kay did just that and sent the synopsis to John Hay "Jock" Whitney, the president of Pioneer and chairman of the board of Selznick

International. After reading the synopsis, Whitney wired Selznick that he would buy the film rights if Selznick didn't.

That was all Selznick needed to hear. On July 7, 1936, only one week after the book's official publication date, Selznick cabled Kay Brown and instructed her to close the deal for the film rights to *GWTW* for $50,000—a record amount for a first novel by an unknown author. Selznick then left on a vacation cruise to Hawaii accompanied by his wife and a copy of *GWTW*. While reading the book during the long days at sea, Selznick realized for the first time the monumental task ahead of him: translating the 1,037 pages of the novel into a workable movie script.

THE MOVIE MOGULS SELZNICK BESTED WITH HIS *GWTW* BUY

Other film studios had the opportunity to buy the film rights to *GWTW*, but Selznick International was the first one to make the best offer to Macmillan. To see who David O. bested with his *GWTW* buy, match the movie mogul in column I to the studio with which he was associated in column II.

COLUMN I	COLUMN II
1. Pandro S. Berman	a. Warner Brothers Pictures
2. Harry Cohn	b. Paramount Pictures
3. Louis B. Mayer	c. Twentieth Century Fox
4. Jack L. Warner	d. MGM
5. Darryl Zanuck	e. RKO
6. Adolph Zukor	f. Columbia Pictures

GABLE GRUMBLES AND SELZNICK SEARCHES

◆

ACTORS WHO WERE CONSIDERED FOR RHETT BUTLER

Warner Baxter
Ronald Colman
Gary Cooper
Errol Flynn
Fredric March
Basil Rathbone

HOW SELZNICK GOT HIS RHETT BUTLER

When the news broke that Selznick International would be making *GWTW* into a movie, the public flooded the studio's offices with mail. Fans of the novel all across the country wrote to Selznick stating their choices for the casting of the major roles.

For the role of Rhett Butler, stars such as Ronald Colman and Fredric March had their supporters, but the name of Clark Gable dominated the pack from the very beginning. Soon movie magazines even got into the act with The Great Casting Battle of *Gone With the Wind*. The October 1937 issue of *Photoplay*, for example, featured a portrait of Gable as Rhett Butler dressed in a black antebellum coat and characterized him in the role as "cool, impertinent, utterly charming." The magazine admitted, "We like all the other handsome actors mentioned as Rhett—only we don't want them as Rhett. We want Gable."

Selznick wanted Gable, too. He was Number One on Selznick's list of actors for the role, followed by Gary Cooper and Errol Flynn. But there was one obstacle standing in the way of offering the part to Gable: Louis B. Mayer, Selznick's father-in-law and the head of Metro-Goldwyn-Mayer. Mayer had Gable under exclusive contract, and Selznick knew that L.B. would demand a heavy price for Gable's services. So despite the overwhelming public clamor for Gable, Selznick decided to look elsewhere for his male star.

For months, Selznick worked hard to secure Gary Cooper for the role. Cooper, though, was under contract to Sam Goldwyn, a friend of Selznick's. Friend or no friend, Goldwyn was unwilling to lend his hot property to another producer.

When Warner Brothers learned of Selznick's interest in their star Errol Flynn, Jack L. Warner offered Selznick a package deal. Besides Flynn for the role of Rhett Butler, Warner agreed to lend Bette Davis for the role of Scarlett and Olivia de Havilland for the role of Melanie. Davis, however, refused to play opposite Flynn, and the offer fell through. Selznick, now back to square one, knew he had to deal with Mayer.

The terms of the deal struck in June 1938 were dear. Louis B. Mayer, after all, didn't have just the ace that Selznick needed; Mayer held the whole deck. As part of the deal, MGM agreed to lend Gable to Selznick as well as to contribute half of the projected $2.5 million production cost of the film. In return, MGM demanded exclusive distribution rights to *GWTW* plus fifty percent of the film's profits. Selznick had no choice but to agree. Unexpectedly, though, a hitch occurred that even Selznick could not have anticipated. Gable wanted nothing to do with the role of Rhett Butler.

Why Gable Hated the Role He Was Born to Play

"I don't want the part for money, chalk, or marbles," Gable told Selznick. Why would Gable resist taking on the role he was born to play, the role the public demanded he play?

"I was scared when I discovered that I had been cast by the public," Gable explained. "I felt that every reader would have a different idea as to how Rhett should be played on the screen, and I didn't see how I could please everybody."

Gable had always been plagued by insecurities about his acting talent. That was why MGM had sought similar roles for him in all his films, lots of rough-and-tumble action but not much emotion.

THE KOBAL COLLECTION/MGM

SCARLETT, RHETT, AND MELANIE IN THE ATLANTA BAZAAR SCENE.

The exception to this was *Parnell*. Gable was still smarting from his portrayal of the Irish Nationalist. A costume drama, *Parnell* was a disaster with fans and critics alike. That made Gable leery of making another historical picture.

Additionally, MGM had always teamed Gable up with directors who could support and guide Gable's masculine image. But that wouldn't be the case with *GWTW*. Portraying Rhett Butler would make demands on Gable he did not think he could meet, and Selznick had tapped George Cukor as the director of the film. Gable knew Cukor's reputation in Hollywood as a woman's director. His fear was that Cukor would focus totally on the roles of Scarlett and Melanie, leaving Gable as Rhett Butler on his own without direction.

Gable was determined not to do the film for love or money. But in the end, he did it for both.

Love and Money Change Gable's Mind

Clark Gable was a married man in love. Although legally separated, he was married to Ria Langham Gable, his second wife. However, he

21

was in love with Carole Lombard, the gifted actress-comedienne. Gable had sought a divorce, but his wife, who was seventeen years his senior, had refused. She was convinced the affair would soon blow over. But the Gable-Lombard romance flourished under the tolerant eye of the movie industry.

Why was Gable so in love with Lombard? She was sexy, funny, and young—age thirty to Gable's thirty-seven. He found in her an extraordinary companion, far different from the two middle-aged women he had married. Lombard had a joyously unrestrained personality, and Gable never knew what she would do next. She might send him a ham with his picture on it or "indulge" his love of cars with a junkyard jalopy painted red and white for Valentine's Day. A selfless, caring person, she anticipated his needs and even shed her glamour-girl image to hunt, fish, and ride with him. Lombard was a heady intoxicant to Gable, and her high-spiritedness was a perfect counterpoint to his serious nature. They loved each other passionately, and their romance was electric with that passion.

One who watched the affair with particular interest was Gable's boss, Louis B. Mayer. All studio bosses were concerned with the public images of their stars, but Mayer had a more important reason for monitoring Gable's love life. Mayer wanted his studio to play a part in *GWTW*'s production, but he had already heard Gable's grumblings concerning the Rhett Butler role. If Gable refused the role, Mayer could suspend him; that was in Gable's contract. What Mayer needed was a bargaining chip to ensure that Gable would not turn down the role. He found that bargaining chip in Ria Gable.

Mrs. Gable saw, via the newspapers, the deepening love between Gable and the beautiful, blonde Carole Lombard. Gossip was rampant in the Hollywood tabloids that the lovers were planning to marry. Eventually, Ria Gable accepted the fact that she would never get her husband back. And that's what Louis B. Mayer had been waiting to hear. He then secretly encouraged Mrs. Gable to ask for an exorbitant divorce settlement. Mayer believed that if Gable were desperate for money, he wouldn't dare risk suspension by refusing the Rhett Butler role.

The divorce would cost Gable plenty: $286,000, plus income taxes on the settlement. A frugal man by nature, Gable probably howled when he learned the terms of the divorce. But he would do anything to marry Lombard, the woman who had captured his heart. Mayer generously offered Gable a $100,000 bonus to sweeten the Rhett Butler deal, and Gable had no choice. Love and money had changed his mind.

On August 25, 1938 Gable forced a smile as L.B. Mayer, with David

O. Selznick looking on, signed the contracts that lent Gable to Selznick International for *GWTW*.

STAR TRACKS: CLARK GABLE

- Born on February 1, 1901 in Cadiz, Ohio.

- Parents: William H. Gable, a wildcatter in the oil-drilling business, and Addie Hershelman Gable, a farmer's daughter who died nine months after her son was born. Two years later, Will Gable married Jennie Dunlap, a milliner and a dressmaker.

- Dropped out of Edinburgh High School after two years and moved to Akron, where he found a job at the Firestone Tire and Rubber factory.

- Fell under the spell of the theater district and worked as an unpaid gofer for an Akron stock company, the Pauline Maclean Players.

- Worked his way to Hollywood in 1924, where he found work as a movie extra.

- Married his first wife, Josephine Dillon (a drama coach) in 1924.

- Attracted the attention of filmmakers with his stage work as Killer Mears in the Los Angeles production of *The Last Mile*.

- Starred in his first feature film, *The Painted Desert*, in 1931. To get the part in this William Boyd western, Gable told the director he knew how to ride. He had never been on a horse in his life. He hired an ex-cowboy to teach him, and by the time the film started two weeks later, Gable was an old hand in the saddle.

- On the basis of a screen test arranged by Lionel Barrymore, Gable signed a short-term contract with Metro-Goldwyn-Mayer in 1930.

- Erupted on the screen in 1931's *A Free Soul*, starring Norma Shearer. The public reacted by sending thousands of fan letters to Gable, and movie magazines declared, "The Great American Male Has Hit the Screen at Last."

- MGM renewed Gable's contract and featured him opposite many of the screen's most desirable women, including Joan Crawford, Greta Garbo, Jean Harlow, Marion Davies, and Myrna Loy.

- Married his second wife, Maria Franklin Prentiss Lucas Langham— a wealthy Texas socialite—in 1931.

- First met Carole Lombard, the love of his life, when they worked together on the film *No Man of Her Own* in 1932.

• Was lent out to Columbia Pictures for the screwball comedy *It Happened One Night*. Gable, in one scene, unbuttoned his shirt and revealed that he was not wearing an undershirt. Taking Gable's cue, millions of American men apparently believed it was more manly not to wear an undershirt. Within a year, sales of undershirts plummeted by seventy-five percent, and garment executives blasted Gable for causing the near ruination of the undershirt industry.

• Won the 1934 Academy Award as Best Actor for *It Happened One Night*.

• Was reluctant to play Fletcher Christian in *Mutiny on the Bounty* because he thought audiences would think he was a sissy in knickers and a pigtail.

• Was nominated for but lost the Academy Award for Best Actor in 1935 for *Mutiny on the Bounty*.

• Was officially elected "The King of Hollywood" in a contest conducted by Ed Sullivan, movie columnist for the *Chicago Tribune-New York Daily News* Syndicated in 1937. Twenty million votes were cast by the public.

• Was signed to play Rhett Butler in *GWTW* in August 1938.

PROBLEMS ON TOP OF PROBLEMS

In 1936 when Selznick bought the rights to *GWTW*, he realized he would be foolhardy to rush into production. Millions were currently reading the novel; characters and scenes were fresh in readers' minds.

Given the novel's monumental size, Selznick knew that translating the story to manageable film footage would involve lengthy cuts. But Selznick also knew the woe that could befall a producer who eliminated a favorite scene or a memorable line of dialogue. Readers would remember and would never forgive him for tampering with Margaret Mitchell's epic. Selznick's plan was to allow a healthy dose of time to dim readers' memories of the book's characters and events.

A circumstance that further delayed production was the deal for Gable. As part of that arrangement, MGM demanded exclusive distribution rights to *GWTW*. But Selznick had a contract with United Artists to release his films through the end of 1938. That meant Selznick couldn't begin filming *GWTW* until early 1939.

How could Selznick possibly hold the public's interest in *GWTW* for the three years it would take to get the film into the movie houses?

To compound his problem, he also had to find a leading lady equal to the task of portraying the fiery Scarlett. But David O. Selznick was a genius; he decided to kill two birds with one stone.

HUMDINGER OF A HOAX: THE SEARCH FOR SCARLETT

Selznick's solution to his dilemma was pure genius, and pure hype. His idea was to launch a nationwide search for an unknown actress to play Scarlett O'Hara.

Selznick had no illusions that the search would actually discover a suitable actress. His only aim was publicity, and lots of it. What better way to keep the country's attention on *GWTW* than by offering America's secretaries, store clerks, and hope-filled starlets the chance to audition for the most coveted role in Tinseltown. What better way to keep reporters and columnists turning out copy about the movie than by providing the media with material for a potential Cinderella story.

Selznick had the perfect accomplice for his hoax. Russell "Bird" Birdwell, Selznick's publicity director, was a master at dreaming up publicity stunts that turned into front-page news for the studio. For the release of *The Garden of Allah*, for example, Birdwell convinced the book's author, Robert Hichens, to invite the recently abdicated King Edward VIII and Wallis Simpson to spend their honeymoon at his Egyptian villa, the Garden of Allah. Newspapers reported the story as a sidebar to the ongoing coverage of the abdication.

In orchestrating the bogus search for Scarlett, Birdwell lost no time in heralding the news. He arranged a press conference to make the announcement and then dispatched three talent scouts to scour the country. Oscar Serlin covered the North and East, Maxwell Arnow headed South with director George Cukor, and Charles Morrison went West.

And while all of America went into a Scarlett frenzy, Selznick turned his attention to the real search: finding his Scarlett among Hollywood's established stars.

ACTRESSES WHO WERE CONSIDERED FOR SCARLETT

Jean Arthur
Lucille Ball
Tallulah Bankhead
Joan Bennett
Claudette Colbert
Joan Crawford
Bette Davis
Irene Dunne
Joan Fontaine
Paulette Goddard
Jean Harlow
Susan Hayward
Katharine Hepburn
Miriam Hopkins
Carole Lombard
Norma Shearer
Ann Sheridan
Margaret Sullavan
Lana Turner
Loretta Young

Moments to Remember in the Search for Scarlett

• Selznick was forced to hire extra security personnel when would-be Scarletts began crashing the studio gates and applying for the role in person.

• On Christmas morning 1937 Selznick discovered a gaily wrapped and beribboned seven-foot-high box outside his front door. When he tore the paper from this supersized surprise, he found a dust-jacketed replica of the *GWTW* novel. Out of the book stepped a young woman dressed in a hoopskirted gown who announced, "Merry Christmas, Mr. Selznick! I am your Scarlett O'Hara."

• While in Atlanta on a talent scouting expedition, director George Cukor's train was attacked by a bevy of costumed belles all demanding movie contracts. One of the belles, known as Honey Chile, was particularly persistent.

She raced through the train's corridors opening stateroom doors in search of the director. In her wake, she managed to disturb honeymooning couples, sleeping children, and gentlemen who were relaxing sans their trousers. Cukor was hiding on the train during the uproar. His assistant, John Darrow, caught up with the agitated actress when she left the sleeping cars to search the platform. With some fast talking, he convinced her that Cukor had gone on to New Orleans by car and that it was futile to pursue him. He detained her until the whistle blew and the train began pulling out of the station. Then he leapt aboard and rejoined Cukor for the next leg of their journey.

The Brightest Stars Vied for Scarlett

Selznick could choose his Scarlett from the brightest stars in the Hollywood firmament. Here's how the major contenders faired:

Bette Davis Ms. Davis pulled in 40 percent of the public's write-in vote as the actress to play Scarlett. Warner Brothers offered Selznick a package deal of Davis as Scarlett and Errol Flynn as Rhett Butler. But Davis refused to star with the dashing swashbuckler. Warner Brothers would not substitute another actor for Flynn, the deal fell through, and Davis's chances to play Scarlett ended. However, that did not stop Davis from playing *another* Southern vixen.

Tallulah Bankhead The Alabama-born Tallulah Bankhead was better known for her work on the London and Broadway stages than for her work in films. But she was a former inamorata of Jock Whitney, and she became the first actress Selznick tested for the role of Scarlett.

Selznick was not impressed with the thirty-four-year-old actress's portrayal of the youthful Scarlett, but the flamboyant, husky-voiced Bankhead was convincing as the more mature Scarlett. Characterizing her tests as "very promising indeed," Selznick told Bankhead that although he considered her "a definite possibility," he wanted to leave his decision open for the time being.

Louella Parsons used her column to warn Selznick about Bankhead's unpopularity: "George Cukor, her friend, is going to direct [the film]. Jock Whitney, another friend, is backing it. So I'm afraid she'll get the part. If she does I personally will go home and weep because she is not Scarlett O'Hara in my language, and if David O. Selznick gives her the part he will have to answer to every man, woman and child in America."

Parsons needn't have worried. Selznick eventually decided that Bankhead was not his Scarlett. He did think, though, that she would make a perfect Belle Watling. Since he had rejected her for the lead, however, he was afraid to approach the explosive Bankhead with his latest inspiration. This task he delegated to Kay Brown. But he cautioned her: "For God's sake, don't mention my name in connection with it, simply saying that it is an idea of your own that you haven't yet taken up with me." But Brown considered it the better part of valor not to mention the idea at all to Bankhead.

Miriam Hopkins   Like Bankhead, Miriam Hopkins was a daughter of the South. Hopkins had recently played the title role in *Becky Sharp*, and her characterization of Thackeray's willful heroine drew Selznick's attention. Instead of testing Hopkins, Selznick screened *Becky Sharp*, and he had Hopkins read for the role of Scarlett. Her intensity in the reading impressed Selznick, but she wasn't quite what he was looking for.

Norma Shearer   The thirty-seven-year-old widow of Irving Thalberg was anxious for the part, but Selznick thought her too mature to play sixteen-year-old Scarlett. Nonetheless, her legions of fans equaled box-office draw and a force Selznick could not afford to ignore. So Selznick decided to test the waters. He leaked to columnist Walter Winchell that Shearer was being considered for the role. When Winchell announced the news to his radio audience, pandemonium ensued! Shearer's fans responded in outraged letters that castigated Selznick for even thinking of asking the gentle, dignified Shearer to play the impetuous, fiery Scarlett. Shortly thereafter, Shearer withdrew her name from consideration for the role.

Katharine Hepburn   When she read the novel, Hepburn knew she was Scarlett O'Hara. Unfortunately, RKO turned down the opportunity to buy the film rights because they felt the part was not right for her. When she learned that Selznick had acquired the film rights and that Cukor would be directing, Hepburn felt she still had a shot at it. She had worked successfully with both Selznick and Cukor in *A Bill of Divorcement* in 1932.

Cukor, however, was not convinced Hepburn was the right choice. Selznick was more direct in his reaction to her candidacy: "I can't imagine Rhett Butler chasing you for ten years." But Hepburn was tenacious. She offered herself as a standby in case Selznick's search for Scarlett turned up empty.

Later, Cukor changed his mind about Hepburn. He had just finished working with her on the film *Holiday* and extolled her acting gifts to Selznick. Selznick ordered a test of her in the role of Scarlett, but Hepburn refused. She insisted that by now Selznick knew if she could act or not. Unfortunately, Selznick was also aware of Hepburn's current unpopularity among film distributors. In 1938 after a series of commercial flops such as *Mary of Scotland*, *A Woman Rebels*, and *Quality Street*, Hepburn was tagged Box Office Poison. Despite this, Selznick felt he couldn't eliminate Hepburn from the running just yet.

Paulette Goddard Ms. Goddard was Selznick's strongest contender for the role of Scarlett. In her test she personified Selznick's image of Scarlett: a dark beauty with a bold and fiery personality. Goddard was inexperienced as an actress though. Selznick signed Goddard to a five-year contract, hired a coach to refine her talents, and sent her for training to develop a Southern accent. Another test confirmed to Selznick just how good Goddard was, and it seemed as if she had the role wrapped up. Columnist Louella Parsons even began referring to her as "Scarlett O'Goddard." But a hitch developed.

Goddard was the protégée of Charles Chaplin. She had costarred in his film *Modern Times* and was currently starring in the role of the third Mrs. Chaplin. Although the pair lived together, there was widespread disbelief about their married status. When women's clubs across the country learned that Goddard was about to be signed for the role of Scarlett, Selznick was deluged with letters of protest. The public was not only furious over a suspected immoral liaison but provoked as well by the left-wing views Chaplin had exhibited in *Modern Times*.

Goddard assured Selznick that she and Chaplin had been married aboard an anchored yacht in the harbor of Singapore during a cruise to the Orient. Selznick demanded to see the marriage license. Goddard countered that the yacht had been attacked by guerrillas and all the records destroyed. Rather than risk censure—and boycott—of his film by an outraged public, Selznick decided to continue looking for his Scarlett.

Jean Arthur Charmingly original at thirty-three years of age, Jean Arthur was a sentimental favorite for Selznick. He and Arthur had been a Hollywood item before he married Louis B. Mayer's daughter Irene. Arthur's early readings had a magic quality, and although she clearly was not a Southern belle, Selznick seriously considered her for the role.

Joan Bennett Ms. Bennett had been a rising star with lovely blonde looks and a fine performance in *Little Women* to her credit. After she wore a black wig for her role in *Trade Winds*, her stunning appearance convinced her to remain a brunette and to audition for Scarlett. Selznick was equally impressed with the new Bennett. He offered her an opportunity to read for the role of Scarlett, but she insisted on a screen test. After he viewed the test, Selznick decided Bennett was a serious contender for the role.

Lesser Luminaries Also Had a Chance to Shine

Other rising stars in the Hollywood galaxy had the opportunity to read and test for Scarlett O'Hara. They included the following:

Lana Turner "Sweater Girl" Lana was one of the newest sex symbols when she tested for Scarlett. She had played a Southern girl in Warner's *They Won't Forget*, a 1937 film people were still talking about. Turner's Scarlett screen test had her paired with Melvyn Douglas playing Ashley. But Selznick found her "completely inadequate, too young to have a grasp of the part."

Susan Hayward According to Hollywood legend, Irene Mayer Selznick spotted attractive, redheaded, nineteen-year-old Edythe Marrener modeling hats in a New York fashion show. Marrener traveled to Hollywood and tested for Scarlett. Although her performance was stiff and unprofessional, Selznick gave her a six-month contract. He used her as a Scarlett stand-in during tests for other roles. At the end of her contract period, Selznick dismissed Marrener. Undaunted, Marrener changed her name to Susan Hayward, won a contract from Paramount, and enjoyed a successful Hollywood film career.

Ann Sheridan Selznick had heard fabulous things about Ann Sheridan. A relative newcomer, she had an amazing string of hits at Warner Brothers, and Selznick was worried about passing up an actress with great potential. Under close scrutiny, though, Sheridan's talents failed to impress Selznick.

Lucille Ball To leave no stone unturned, Selznick offered Scarlett tryouts to actresses under contract to other studios. RKO rounded up eight of its stock girls, handed them scripts containing three scenes from *GWTW*, and told them to be ready for auditions in three weeks. One of the stock girls, redheaded Lucille Ball, knew she could never be Scarlett O'Hara. But rather than balk and risk losing her RKO contract, she started memorizing her lines.

On her way to the afternoon audition, Ball was caught in a freak cloudburst. She arrived at Selznick's office thoroughly soaked. Selznick had not yet arrived, so the bedraggled Ball was ushered into the producer's office and told to wait. She knelt in front of the blazing fireplace to dry herself and decided to practice her lines.

Moments later she was startled at the sound of Selznick's voice complimenting her on her reading. She was aghast at his finding her rehearsing, but he urged her to continue. Summoning all her strength, she completed her scenes. Selznick said he enjoyed her reading, thanked her for coming, and then helped her to her feet. Only then did Ball realize she had auditioned for the Scarlett O'Hara role on her knees.

Lucille Ball made a name for herself as a madcap comedienne in the years that followed her disastrous audition. When she and her husband Desi Arnaz were looking for a location to produce their *I Love Lucy* television series, they bought the old Selznick studio. And which office did Ball choose for herself? Selznick's old one.

CASTING CALL

◆

MARGARET MITCHELL: AN INNOCENT BYSTANDER IN THE *GWTW* CASTING BATTLE

Margaret Mitchell was emphatic. She wanted absolutely, positively nothing to do with the casting of *GWTW*, and she made this perfectly clear when she sold the film rights to Selznick. The only problem was nobody listened to her. And during the two years it took Selznick to select his stars, Margaret found herself involved, to her great consternation, in the *GWTW* casting battle.

People stopped her on the street, phoned her, wrote to her. When that didn't work, they appeared at her apartment to voice their opinion about the casting of the major roles or to beg for a part in the film. One woman conned Margaret into letting her into her apartment. Once inside, the woman announced she was an actress, smeared dark makeup on her face, and began portraying Mammy in the middle of Margaret's living room.

Margaret probably pulled her hair out when she read Louella Parson's October 23, 1936 column. In the column Parsons wrote: "These rumors of a cast for 'Gone With the Wind' are gradually getting David Selznick down . . . No one has yet been chosen and will not be until the author, Margaret Mitchell, is consulted."

That prompted a lengthy letter to Parsons from Margaret. "Everybody in the world reads your column and that is why I am appealing to you for assistance," Margaret wrote. She begged the columnist to publish a notice stating that Margaret had nothing at all to do with the casting.

Parsons came to Margaret's rescue in her November 8 column in which she quoted Margaret's letter at length. The disturbances to Margaret's private life subsided, at least for awhile.

Another incident that dragged Margaret into the fray occurred in October 1938. Mrs. Ogden Reid, vice president of the *New York Herald Tribune*, phoned Margaret and invited her to the Eighth Annual Women's Forum on Current Problems that was being held in New York. Because of family illness, Margaret declined. Mrs. Reid mentioned that Katharine Hepburn was to be the guest speaker and asked Margaret's opinion of the actress. Margaret commented that she had enjoyed Hepburn's performance in *Little Women* and thought she looked attractive in hoopskirts. Little did she realize how those innocent words would be twisted.

At the forum, Mrs. Reid introduced Hepburn as "my candidate for Scarlett O'Hara in *Gone With the Wind*" and added that the actress also had Margaret Mitchell's endorsement. The 3,000 women in attendance erupted into a standing ovation.

In Atlanta, Margaret was besieged with phone calls from reporters all over the country asking for a statement about her endorsement of Katharine Hepburn. Margaret, stunned at the misinterpretation of her comments, told all who called, "I have never expressed a preference, and I never will."

The press was still not satisfied and hounded Margaret whenever a new contender for Scarlett was announced in Hollywood. "Life has been awful since I sold the movie rights!", she lamented to Kay Brown. Margaret was convinced her quiet, peaceful life was permanently gone with the wind.

Margaret Mitchell's *GWTW* Choices

As much as she sought to avoid entering the Great Casting Battle, it appears that Margaret did express her casting preferences, once and only once. In a July 1936 letter to Macmillan's editor Lois Cole, Margaret noted that "Miriam Hopkins has been my choice for Scarlett from the beginning." For Melanie, she liked Elizabeth Allan, who was known for her recent film portrayal of David Copperfield's mother. "I wish Charles Boyer didn't have a French accent for he's my choice for Rhett," Margaret added. "Next to him, Jack Holt [a Western actor] is the only person I can think of."

WARNER BROTHERS' JEZEBEL REVENGE

In the vernacular, a "jezebel" is a shameless woman. In Selznick's mind *Jezebel*, the 1938 Warner Brothers film starring Bette Davis, was a shameless imitation of *GWTW*. And Selznick was furious.

After the deal fell through to have Bette Davis portray Scarlett, Warner Brothers bought the rights to the 1933 play *Jezebel*. Set in pre–Civil War years, the drama concerned the machinations of a strong-willed Southern vixen very much in character like Scarlett O'Hara. Years earlier, Davis had encouraged her employers to make the purchase when the play was appearing on Broadway. But the production turned out to be a dismal failure, and no studio was interested in the movie rights. However, now that *GWTW* was the talk of the country, Warner Brothers snapped up *Jezebel* and rushed the film into production.

Bette Davis played the unbelievably bitchy title role, and the film was shot in less than eight weeks. During the filming, vice-president in charge of production Jack Warner called the press's attention to the similarities between his studio's film and *GWTW*. Warner noted that on the set Davis was known as "Scarlett." In interviews Davis commented on the parallels between the characters.

This was enough to set Selznick off. After previewing *Jezebel*, he sent a telegram to Warner warning that "it would be a very great pity indeed . . . if so distinguished and costly a picture as *Jezebel* should be damned as an imitation by the millions of readers and lovers of *Gone with the Wind*.

Selznick noted that *Jezebel* was "permeated with characterizations, attitudes, and scenes that unfortunately resemble *Gone With the Wind*." He cited one scene in which men, gathered around a dinner table, discuss the threat of war and the North's military advantages over the South. "This scene is lifted practically bodily out of *Gone With the Wind*," Selznick charged. The scene was later dropped from *Jezebel*.

In closing, Selznick stated that he thought it was important "that the success which your picture deserves should not be marred by any appearance of an attempt to capitalize on a work for which the American public has demonstrated such a great love."

The American public that loved *GWTW* also loved *Jezebel*. The film was wildly successful. And almost a year before *GWTW* even made its film debut, Davis's memorable performance in *Jezebel* won her an Academy Award, her second. To say the least, Selznick was not pleased.

THE BOGUS SEARCH PAYS OFF

By the time the two-year search for Scarlett ended, the stunt had cost Selznick nearly $92,000. Nearly 149,000 feet of black-and-white film and 13,000 feet of Technicolor film had been shot in tests of 1,400 aspiring Scarletts. And the resulting national publicity was all that Selznick had hoped for.

Surprisingly, though, the search did uncover three actresses, all Southern belles, who captured secondary roles in *GWTW*. Marcella Martin from Shreveport, Louisiana won the role of Cathleen Calvert; Mary Anderson from Birmingham, Alabama was selected for Maybelle Merriwether; and Alicia Rhett from Charleston, South Carolina was to play India Wilkes.

DETERMINED DE HAVILLAND
CAPTURES THE ROLE OF MELANIE

RKO actress Joan Fontaine received a message that George Cukor wanted her to read for *GWTW*. Oh, what she wouldn't give to play Scarlett! But when she arrived for her appointment, she discovered that the director had her in mind for Melanie. Since that role held no interest for her, she suggested that Cukor test her sister, Olivia de Havilland.

De Havilland was hungry for Melanie. And she knew that her competition was stiff: Elizabeth Allan, Andrea Leeds, Ann Shirley, and Frances Dee had tested for the role. She read for the part at Cukor's office, and he suggested that she read for Selznick.

Several days later, de Havilland replayed the same scene in Selznick's house with Cukor taking the role of Scarlett. When de Havilland finished, Selznick decided that she *was* Melanie and offered her the role on the spot. She was joyous, but then her emotions crashed to the floor. Jack L. Warner would never let her accept the part.

De Havilland was a contract player at Warner Brothers. When her career began there in the '30s, she was cast opposite handsome Errol Flynn. The combination worked. Dashing Flynn and doe-eyed de Havilland starred in a string of hero-rescues-damsel-in-distress films from *Captain Blood* to *Robin Hood*. But as Flynn's career soared, de Havilland's seemed permanently grounded.

Under her contract, de Havilland had to appear in any film to which she was assigned. If she refused any role, she could be immediately suspended without pay. And under the studio system, which indentured its stars to multiyear contracts, suspension was professional suicide.

Also against her was the star system at Warner's, which favored male actors such as Cagney, Robinson, and Bogart. Plus, the reigning queen of the lot, Bette Davis, was not easily dethroned. So there really was no place for de Havilland's career to go unless she sought roles outside the studio. And this, according to Jack L. Warner, was verboten.

True to his dictates, Warner's response was a resounding "no" when de Havilland approached him about taking on the role. He also feared that once de Havilland had a taste of freedom she would be unwilling to return to the shackles of the studio system.

But Warner underestimated demure de Havilland. Rather than accept Warner's verdict as the final word, this iron-willed magnolia decided to appeal to someone who could change her boss's mind: his wife.

De Havilland invited Mrs. Warner for tea at the Beverly Hills Brown Derby and poured out the details of her plight. Mrs. Warner, a former actress, was sympathetic and pledged to do what she could. With such a powerful force at work, Jack L. Warner soon capitulated.

As part of the deal for de Havilland, Selznick agreed to lend new star James Stewart for use in the Warner film *No Time for Comedy*. Warner thought he would profit from the deal, but the price he eventually paid for lending out de Havilland was incalculable.

Warner was right that de Havilland would be difficult to work with after she found stardom outside the studio. What he could not have anticipated was her leading a rebellion when she returned to the Warner lot. Her challenge to Jack Warner's authority moved from the lot, through the California court system, and ended with the destruction of the very studio system he controlled.

Star Tracks: Olivia de Havilland

• Born on July 1, 1916 in Tokyo, Japan.

• Parents: Walter and Lillian Ruse de Havilland. Walter was a professor of law at the Waseda University in Tokyo. Their marriage broke up after the birth of a second child, Joan, in 1917. Afterwards, Lillian returned to America, settled with her daughters in Saratoga, California, and later married George Fontaine.

• Original career goal was to become a teacher.

• Portrayed Puck in a 1934 local production of *A Midsummer Night's Dream*, which caught the eye of a talent scout. The talent scout represented producer Max Reinhardt, who was planning to begin a national tour of the play at the Hollywood Bowl. De Havilland traveled to Hollywood to audition and was selected as second understudy to the actress playing Hermia. Before opening night, the actress and her first understudy were called to make a motion picture, leaving de Havilland to undertake the role. In front of a star-studded audience, de Havilland triumphed.

• Her opening-night performance was seen by a producer at Warner Brothers who convinced Jack Warner to fly out from New York to see de Havilland. Warner Brothers was planning a film version of the play. Warner attended the last night of the performance, was impressed with de Havilland, and offered her a long-term contract.

• Was cast in some forgettable Warner Brothers productions: *Alibi Ike, The Irish in Us, Hard to Get.*

• Began playing opposite newcomer Errol Flynn in films such as *Captain Blood* and *The Charge of the Light Brigade.* She became infatuated with the handsome but reckless actor.

• Was cast as Angela Giusseppi in *Anthony Adverse* (1936). She played opposite Fredric March.

• Used her iron will and determination to capture the role of Melanie in *GWTW* after Jack Warner refused to lend her to Selznick International.

THE WINNING OVER OF LESLIE HOWARD

For Selznick, Leslie Howard was the perfect Ashley Wilkes. Howard was known for his portrayals of intelligent, introspective, and idealistic characters in films such as *Of Human Bondage, The Petrified Forest,* and *Pygmalion.*

For Howard, playing Ashley was perfect nonsense. "I haven't the slightest intention of playing another weak, watery character such as Ashley Wilkes," he told Selznick. "I've played enough ineffectual characters already."

Howard's refusal stunned Selznick. Any one of the actresses he was considering for Scarlett could handle that role, but finding another actor to play Ashley was impossible. Howard was Ashley.

In the light of Howard's refusal, Selznick tested Melvyn Douglas and found him "much too beefy physically" for the delicate Ashley. At his wife Irene's suggestion, Selznick tested Ray Milland. Milland,

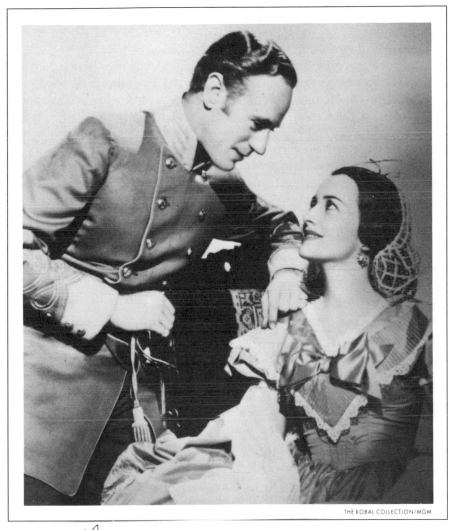

THE KOBAL COLLECTION/MGM

LESLIE HOWARD AS ASHLEY WILKES AND
OLIVIA DE HAVILLAND AS HIS WIFE, MELANIE.

however, couldn't quite master the Southern accent. For awhile, Selznick even considered newcomer Jeffrey Lynn, but he was rejected as well.

"I think it extremely unlikely that we will find any Ashley that will be as satisfactory to me, or that any of the Ashleys that we are testing will prove on film to be as right as Leslie Howard seems to be in my imagination," Selznick confided to an associate.

Howard was adamant, though. At forty-five, he felt uncomfortable playing the youthful Ashley. He also felt that accepting the role would continue the typecasting he had grown to hate.

Selznick was now faced with the task of winning over Leslie Howard. Unlike Gable, Howard could not be seduced by money. But Selznick knew of Howard's longing to produce or direct films; what might appeal to Howard, then, would be the chance to escape behind the camera. Selznick decided to make the actor an enticing offer. If Howard would accept the role of Ashley, Selznick would give him the opportunity to star in and be the associate producer of Selznick's next film, *Intermezzo*. The prospect was utterly irresistible, and Howard signed on the dotted line.

Star Tracks: Leslie Howard

• Born Leslie Howard Stainer on April 3, 1893 in London, England.

• Parents: Frank and Lilian Stainer. His father was an office worker and stockbroker.

• His mother encouraged him to write plays and to act. He wrote and acted while completing his education, but his father discouraged him from entering the acting profession. Howard worked as a banker until World War I interrupted his career.

• Married Ruth Martin in 1916.

• Enlisted in the British army and was sent to the front lines in France. A year later, he was sent home suffering from shell shock.

• Disillusioned with banking, he decided to become an actor. Most stage actors were at this time fighting in the war, so it was relatively easy for him to find work. He began his career on the London stage and used his first and middle names as his stage name. He toured in *Peg O' My Heart* and *Charley's Aunt*.

• Promised his wife in 1917 that if he wasn't successful as an actor in five years, he would quit and become a businessman.

• His son, Ronald, was born in 1918.

• Left London for America in late 1920 to accept a role in the Broadway play *Just Suppose*.

• His daughter, Leslie Ruth, was born in 1924.

• Found success in other American plays: *Outward Bound*, *The Green Hat*, and *Her Cardboard Lover*.

• After his debut in *Her Cardboard Lover* in 1926, the New York

Daily News proclaimed, "Cardboard Lover Belongs to Howard." His star finally shone nine years after the promise he made to his wife.

• Traveled to Hollywood in 1930 to make his first film—*Outward Bound* for Warner Brothers.

• Signed a contact with Metro-Goldwyn-Mayer to make three films in 1931: *Never the Twain Shall Meet, Five and Ten,* and *A Free Soul,* which featured Norma Shearer and Clark Gable.

• Signed a three-year, three-pictures-a-year contract with Warner Brothers in 1933.

• Other films: *Of Human Bondage* (1934); *The Scarlet Pimpernel* (1935); *The Petrified Forest* (1936); *Romeo and Juliet* (1936).

• Originally played in *The Petrified Forest* on Broadway with newcomer Humphrey Bogart in the role of gangster Duke Mantee. When Warner Brothers was casting the film version, Howard was asked to re-create his role, but Warner wanted Edward G. Robinson to take the Bogart role. Howard told Warner Brothers that he would not make the film unless Bogart could re-create his role as well. The Brothers Warner gave in, and Bogart got the role that launched his career.

• Academy Award nominations: Howard was nominated Best Actor of 1932–33 for his role of Peter Standish in the film *Berkeley Square;* nominated Best Actor of 1938 for his role of Professor Henry Higgins in the screen version of *Pygmalion.* He lost both times.

• Signed for the role of Ashley Wilkes in January 1939.

SMALLER ROLES

Gerald O'Hara

There was only one serious contender for the role of Scarlett's father, and that was character actor Thomas Mitchell. Mitchell had originally followed his father's footsteps into a newspaper career, but he soon began writing plays in his spare time and dreamed of becoming an actor. His dream became reality in 1920 when he debuted on Broadway. For fifteen years, he had a triple stage career acting, directing, and writing in numerous plays.

A contract from Columbia Pictures lured Mitchell to Hollywood in 1936. His early credits included *Craig's Wife, Adventure in Manhattan, Theodora Goes Wild,* and *When You're in Love.* In 1937, Mitchell appeared in Frank Capra's *Lost Horizon* and John Ford's *The Hurricane;*

both brought him important attention. For his work in *The Hurricane*, he was nominated for an Academy Award as Best Supporting Actor. That led to three roles that would crown the year 1939 for Mitchell: Doc Boone in Ford's *Stagecoach*, the newspaperman in *Mr. Smith Goes to Washington*, and Gerald O'Hara in *GWTW*.

Ellen O'Hara

Selznick had few choices for the role of Scarlett's mother. He first offered the part to Lillian Gish, but she turned it down. He was considering Cornelia Otis Skinner when he decided on Barbara O'Neil.

Barbara O'Neil began her career on the Broadway stage. From there

THE O'HARA SISTERS WORKING THE FIELDS. CARREEN (ANN RUTHERFORD), SUELLEN (EVELYN KEYES), AND SCARLETT.

she joined a repertory company and met her one-time future husband, director Joshua Logan. Deciding to try films, O'Neil headed for Hollywood in 1937. Her movie roles ranged from the warm second wife in *Stella Dallas* to the awful shrew in *All This, And Heaven Too* for which she received an Oscar nomination. She and Thomas Mitchell played husband and wife in *Love, Honor and Behave*, and her casting as Scarlett's mother in 1939 renewed their working relationship.

Suellen O'Hara

Evelyn Keyes, a native of Port Arthur, Texas, was raised in Atlanta, Georgia. As a teenager, she left Margaret Mitchell's hometown for Hollywood and a film career. Cecil B. DeMille offered her a contract, and she won roles in his films *The Buccaneer* and *Union Pacific*.

When casting *GWTW*, Selznick wrote to a staff member, "I don't know anything about Evelyn Keyes and will be interested to see her." He met her, liked what he saw in the attractive blonde actress, and immediately attempted to lure her to the infamous casting couch. Keyes eluded the pursuing Selznick by running around his large mahogany desk until he had to stop to catch his breath. Then she escaped. But Selznick didn't hold her rebuff against her; he offered her the role of Suellen O'Hara.

Carreen O'Hara

Selznick originally wanted Judy Garland for the role of Scarlett's youngest sister. But Garland accepted the role of Dorothy in *The Wizard of Oz*, which put her out of the running for the small role of Carreen O'Hara. Instead, Selznick turned to Andy Hardy's girlfriend.

Canadian-born Ann Rutherford began her career in radio. She moved on to small roles in films, and then in 1937 was offered a contract by MGM. She is best known for the twelve Andy Hardy movies she made in which she played Mickey Rooney's girlfriend, Polly Benedict.

Mammy

Selznick read that Elizabeth McDuffie, Mrs. Franklin D. Roosevelt's maid, was the star of the White House servants' amateur theater troupe. With Mrs. Roosevelt's permission, Selznick tested McDuffie for the role of Mammy and reaped a harvest of national publicity. More seriously, Selznick tested Hattie Noel and Louise Beavers for the role before he selected Hattie McDaniel.

Hattie McDaniel's career began when she worked as a singer with Professor George Morrison's Orchestra, a black band that toured the country. She was the first black woman to sing on network radio and was soon known as "the colored Sophie Tucker." In 1931, she arrived in Hollywood to seek a film career and began as an extra before capturing larger parts. She is remembered for her roles in *Show Boat*, *Saratoga* (especially for the scene in which she sang with Clark Gable) and *China Seas*. During times when work in films was not available, she hired herself out as a domestic, a cook, or a washerwoman.

Her portrayal of Mammy in *GWTW* brought her fame as well as unexpected criticism. Thereafter, she came under fire for continually accepting movie roles as a stereotypical domestic. But McDaniel pointed to the domestic work she had done during the lean years. Comparing the differences in salaries between working as a domestic and portraying one, McDaniel said she much preferred the film work.

Prissy

Selznick was certain he had a winner with his selection of squeaky-voiced Butterfly McQueen to play Scarlett's addle-brained maid, Prissy.

In 1935, Thelma McQueen moved from her hometown of Tampa, Florida to New York City where she joined a Harlem acting group. She adopted the name Butterfly after dancing the "Butterfly Ballet" in *A Midsummer Night's Dream*. She debuted on Broadway in 1937 in *Brown Sugar* and played in *What a Life!* the following year. In 1939 she was in the Benny Goodman-Louis Armstrong musical *Swingin' On a Dream* when Selznick signed her to play Prissy.

Aunt Pittypat Hamilton

Billie Burke was desperate for the role of Aunt Pittypat. Although Selznick thought she was too young and slim for the part, he agreed to a screen test.

Her costume was stuffed with pounds of padding. Makeup artists fattened her features with a fake double chin and piled cotton stuffing into her cheeks. She waddled onto the set and began her test. Her overabundant padding and the oppressive studio lights conspired against her: She almost keeled over from the heat. Several days after this disastrous test, Selznick signed the more robust Laura Hope Crews for the role.

Laura Hope Crews began acting at the age of four. Her career as a child actress was interrupted by her education, but after high school she left her native San Francisco for the lights of Broadway. She debuted in *Merely Mary Ann* in 1904. During the 1920s she appeared in numerous plays including *Mr. Pim Passes By*, *Merry Wives of Gotham*, *Pomerory's Past*, and *Hay Fever* (which she directed). Following her outstanding performance in *The Silver Cord* in 1926, she was offered the opportunity to travel to Hollywood to coach film stars making the transition from silent films to the talkies.

Her own film career, which had begun in 1929 with *Charming Sinners*, blossomed in the '30s. Highlights included reprising her stage role in the film *The Silver Cord*, playing Prudence in *Camille*, and Aunt Pittypat in *Gone With the Wind*.

Uncle Peter

Selznick originally tested Eddie Anderson for the role of Pork, the O'Haras' house servant, but gravel-voiced Anderson was signed to play the Hamiltons' major domo, Uncle Peter.

Anderson acquired his distinctive voice after he damaged his vocal cords as a twelve-year-old newspaper hawker on the streets of Oakland, California. He soon abandoned that career to join vaudeville and tour in a song and-dance duo with his brother and later as a solo act.

In Hollywood, he found small parts in movies, but his real claim to fame came from radio. His portrayal of the wise-cracking valet Rochester on the *Jack Benny Show* in 1937 kept listeners in stitches.

Anderson appeared in *The Green Pastures* and even though he landed a role in *Jezebel*, Selznick obviously forgave him and used his talents in *GWTW*.

Dr. Meade

Selznick decided on Lionel Barrymore for the role of Dr. Meade in 1937. But by the time *GWTW* was ready for shooting, Barrymore had been stricken with crippling arthritis and was confined to a wheelchair. Lewis Stone, who was known for his role as Andy Hardy's father, was also considered, but Selznick decided on veteran actor Harry Davenport.

Harry Davenport was born in New York City to a theatrical family. So it was not unusual for Davenport's career debut to be on the stage when he was only five. From his vast work in theater, he moved on to motion pictures in 1912 and became an actor and part-time director for New York's Vitagraph Company. He was drawn to Hollywood in the 1930s and quickly established himself as a character actor, recruited for films by all the major studios.

COPYRIGHT 1939 SELZNICK INT'L. PICTURES, INC. REN. 1967 MGM, INC.

SCARLETT WITH DR. MEADE (HARRY DAVENPORT).

Belle Watling

Selznick had wanted to test Tallulah Bankhead, a rejected Scarlett, for the role of Atlanta's madam. But the suggestion was diplomatically ignored. Selznick fleetingly thought Mae West "might be glad to do it as a stunt." He tested Joan Blondell, Loretta Young, and Gladys George, but then he saw Ona Munson.

Ona Munson entered the world of vaudeville in 1922 as a singer and dancer. She toured in the starring role of *No, No, Nanette*, then played the role in the Broadway production. Other plays such as *Manhattan Mary* and *Hold Everything* followed.

The year 1931 found her breaking into films in Hollywood. She had a role in *Five Star Final*, an Edward G. Robinson film that was nominated for an Academy Award as best picture. She continued her work on Broadway during the 1930s and even took her musical and dramatic talents to radio. She played Lorelei in the *Big Town* radio series.

The scene chosen for Munson's *GWTW* test was Belle's encounter with Melanie outside the Atlanta church-turned-hospital. Munson's performance was superb, and Selznick signed her immediately.

Frank Kennedy

The role of Scarlett's second husband went to Carroll Nye, who began his career in the silent film *Classified*. His most noteworthy role before *GWTW* was the romantic lead in 1928's *While the City Sleeps*. Stardom was elusive for Nye for the next ten years, but when the spotlight of *GWTW* shone upon him, he felt he could make a comeback.

Jonas Wilkerson

Robert Gleckler began the role of Jonas Wilkerson, but the actor died of uremic poisoning during production. He was replaced by Victor Jory.

Jory, born in Alaska, pursued an athletic career as a prizefighter and then a champion wrestler before turning his attention to acting. His first film in 1932 led to others in which he was usually cast as a villain. He played Injun Joe in the 1938 Selznick production *The Adventures of Tom Sawyer*.

Stuart Tarleton

Max Arnow, Selznick's casting director, discovered Kentucky-born George Reeves acting in a play at the Pasadena Playhouse in southern California. Reeves was signed to play one of Scarlett's beaux, Stuart Tarleton. On the screen credits, though, he was mistakenly identified as Brent Tarleton.

SELZNICK "FINDS" HIS SCARLETT

◆

THE CONTINUING SAGA OF TRANSFORMING *GWTW* INTO A SCRIPT, Part One

Since Margaret Mitchell refused to have anything to do with turning her novel into a movie script, Selznick had to find a writer equal to the task. He found that someone in Sidney Howard.

Howard, a Pulitzer Prize winner and one of America's leading playwrights, had a reputation for excellence. Not only did he write for the stage (*They Knew What They Wanted, The Silver Cord, Yellow Jacket,* and *Dodsworth*); he also wrote for the screen (*Arrowsmith, Bulldog Drummond,* and *Raffles*).

Howard began working on the *GWTW* script in early 1937, using a copy of the novel that contained Selznick's comments jotted in the margins. Selznick was not happy that Howard preferred to work in New York. "I never had much success with leaving a writer alone to do a script, without almost daily collaboration with myself and usually the director," Selznick complained in a memo to Kay Brown, who had negotiated the deal for Howard.

Howard wrote at a breakneck sixteen-hour-a-day pace and completed the script—all 400 pages of it—in six weeks. He had condensed pages of narration into manageable scenes, eliminated minor characters, and had cut, cut, cut without losing any of the flavor that Margaret Mitchell had imparted.

Selznick was pleased with Howard's work. But the script had a playing time of nearly six hours. For awhile Selznick considered making the film as two pictures, but he changed his mind when he was advised that the format would be unpopular with audiences. So together in California in early 1938, Selznick and Howard hammered out the second, third, and fourth drafts of the script, the two of them discussing the script and Howard doing the actual writing. Howard, feeling that his work was at last finished, then went back to New York.

Selznick, ever the perfectionist, was still not completely satisfied with the script. He put it on a shelf but browsed through it occasionally during the next few months, making notes on areas for revision.

In October 1938, Selznick tried to coax Howard to accompany him on a trip to Bermuda so they could work on the script again. But Howard, the owner of a 700-acre cattle farm in Tyringham, Massachusetts, refused: "I have a cow with calf. I'm not about to leave at this time."

By the end of October, three months before the official date of shooting, Selznick had put Howard's script aside and began thinking about getting another writer to handle the project. (*To be continued . . .*)

THE LONG AND THE SHORT
OF FILMING *GWTW*

According to calculations worked out by Selznick's studio, filming *GWTW* exactly as Margaret Mitchell wrote it would yield a picture 168 hours long. Moviegoers would certainly have had sore bottoms. At that length, it would take a week of straight 24-hours-a-day viewing to see the entire film. Thankfully, Selznick was thinking in realistic terms. He envisioned the film as running between two-and-a-half and three hours.

STAR TRACKS: VIVIEN LEIGH

- Born Vivian Mary Hartley on November 5, 1913 in Darjeeling, India.

- Parents: Ernest Richard Hartley and Gertrude Robinson Yackje. Ernest was a clerk in the brokerage house of Piggott Chapman and Company.

- Received her education in English, French, and Italian convent schools. As a child, she knew she wanted to be an actress. After completing her formal education, she attended London's Royal Academy of Dramatic Art.

- Married Herbert Leigh Holman, an English barrister, in 1932 and welcomed a daughter, Suzanne, the following year.

- First film: *Things Are Looking Up*, a British film in which she had a minor role.

- Adopted the professional name Vivien Leigh by slightly changing the spelling of her given name and borrowing her husband's middle name.

- Her role in the stage production *The Mask of Virtue* (1935) caused a sensation in London and attracted the attention of producer Alexander Korda. He signed her to a contract with London Films.

- Fell in love with Laurence Olivier after seeing him in the play *Theatre Royal*.

- Acted for the first time with Olivier in the film *Fire Over England* (1936). The two were lovers by this time.

- Broke her ankle while skiing in Austria in 1936 and recuperated by reading a recently published first novel entitled *Gone With the Wind*.

- Had the second female lead as an unfaithful wife in the 1938 MGM film *A Yank at Oxford*. She played Elsa Craddock, whose flirtatious behavior nearly gets star Robert Taylor expelled from Oxford.

- Played an East London street entertainer in 1938's *St. Martin's Lane*, which was retitled *The Streets of London* for its American release.

- Captured the coveted role of Scarlett O'Hara in *GWTW*.

SELZNICK DISCOVERS HIS SCARLETT

The Official Story

By December 1938 Selznick had still not found his Scarlett. And time was running out. Selznick had to put Gable to work soon, which meant production could not be delayed any longer. Filming *GWTW* had to begin with or without an actress to play Scarlett O'Hara.

Selznick planned to build Tara on the studio's back lot, which was littered with sets from *The Last of the Mohicans*, *King Kong*, *The Garden of Allah*, and *Little Lord Fauntleroy*. Rather than having them carted away, Selznick decided to reconstruct and repaint the sets to represent Atlanta. He could then torch the old sets to clear the way for the construction of Tara and at the same time film the scene of the burning of the munitions warehouses at the Atlanta depot.

Everything was ready for the night of December 10, 1938. Seven

COPYRIGHT 1939 SELZNICK INT'L. PICTURES, INC. REN. 1967 MGM, INC.

THE BURNING OF THE ATLANTA DEPOT.

Technicolor cameras were positioned to capture the scene at different angles. Three pairs of Rhett and Scarlett doubles were in horse-drawn wagons anticipating their race through the flames. Oil sprinkler pipes were threaded among the sets. Standing by were fire companies from Los Angeles, two hundred studio workers, and various pieces of firefighting equipment just in case the fire got out of control.

Selznick checked his watch as he nervously paced on the platform that rose high above the scene. His mother and a group of friends and colleagues were there to watch the spectacle, and his brother Myron was expected to arrive at any moment. Myron, a Hollywood agent, was dining with clients and had told Selznick that he might be late.

An hour later Myron had still not arrived, and Selznick was told that the firefighters could wait no longer. Reluctantly, he gave the signal, and suddenly Atlanta was ablaze.

As the flames licked the sky, "Action" was called, the cameras began rolling, and the doubles dashed through the inferno. Sparks flew, smoke billowed, and buildings rumbled. A towering brick wall used in *King Kong* groaned then collapsed in a shower of flames. Selznick reveled in the sensational scene.

As the flames died away, a slightly drunk Myron climbed the platform with his guests, actor Laurence Olivier and a beautiful woman wearing a black picture hat and a mink coat. David Selznick was furious with his brother, but his fury melted when he was introduced to Olivier's companion, Vivien Leigh. "I want you to meet Scarlett O'Hara," Myron said.

"The flames were lighting up her face," David Selznick recalled. "I took one look and knew that she was right, at least as far as her appearance went, at least right as far as my conception of how Scarlett O'Hara looked. I'll never recover from that first look."

That first look told Selznick his two-year search was over. Out of the ashes of Atlanta he had finally discovered his Scarlett, according to the official story.

The Real Story

After reading *GWTW* for the first time, Vivien Leigh hungered for the role of Scarlett O'Hara. Her theater colleagues scoffed at the idea of an unknown English actress stepping into a role coveted by most Hollywood actresses. But Leigh would not be dissuaded. She *would* play Scarlett.

She persuaded her agent to submit her name to Selznick International before the American premiere of her film *Fire Over England*, which was produced by Alexander Korda. Kay Brown gave Leigh's name to Selznick in February 1937, who responded, "I have no enthusiasm for Vivien Leigh. Maybe I will have, but as yet have never even seen photograph of her. Will be seeing *Fire Over England* shortly, at which time will of course see Leigh."

Perhaps *Fire Over England* first kindled in Selznick the desire to have Leigh as his Scarlett. His desire blazed with her coquettish performance in 1938's *A Yank at Oxford*. Between February and August 1938, Selznick viewed all of Leigh's British films and studied photographs of her.

Selznick decided to keep Leigh a closely guarded secret. The American public might reject an English woman playing a Southern belle. Plus, the actresses who believed they had a chance to play Scarlett might go for Selznick's jugular were they to find out he was considering someone else all along. There would be less backlash if Leigh's announcement as Scarlett were to come as close as possible to the start of filming.

In secret correspondence, he urged Leigh and Olivier not to end their respective marriages until after the filming of *GWTW* began. Then Selznick began hush-hush negotiations with Alexander Korda, who had Leigh under exclusive contract. But Korda, who had groomed Leigh's acting talents for the prior three years, was initially unwilling to release his special find to Selznick.

By late 1938, though, Korda was beset with financial difficulties and was ready to make a deal. In November, he and Leigh met Selznick in New York, where the producer was staying after his cruise to Bermuda. There they worked out the terms of the deal (contingent, of course, upon Leigh's screen test for the role) and concocted the story they would feed to the press.

According to the official story, Leigh was in the United States hoping to replace Merle Oberon in *Wuthering Heights* and to star opposite Olivier. This was most unlikely since Oberon was under contract to the film's producer, Samuel Goldwyn.

Leigh flew to Hollywood, where Olivier met her at the airport and drove her to the Beverly Hills Hotel. There she kept a low profile until Selznick could stage a proper entrance for her. It was decided that Leigh would "meet" Selznick on December 10, the night Atlanta would go up in flames.

The plan proceeded like clockwork. Leigh and Olivier arrived on the back lot on time, but Myron Selznick was late. David Selznick signaled for the conflagration to begin, and as the last flames lapped at the Atlanta buildings, Myron finally arrived to make his "introduction." And David Selznick's "first look" told him that he had "met" his Scarlett.

VIVIEN LEIGH: THE DARK-HORSE SCARLETT

About 1 A.M., after the flames were no more than dying embers, the Selznick party returned to Selznick's office for a drink. Selznick showed Leigh the scenes from the script to be used for the screen test and asked her to read Scarlett's lines for him and George Cukor.

Leigh felt an immediate rapport with Cukor. He was equally impressed with her. As she ran through the scenes, both Selznick and Cukor were sure she would be the perfect Scarlett. Despite her clipped British tones, Cukor assured Selznick, "I don't think she'll find the Southern accent any trouble."

Two days after Leigh's reading, Selznick sent a letter to his wife: "Saturday I was greatly exhilarated by the Fire Sequence. . . . Myron rolled in just exactly too late, arriving about a minute and a half after the last building had fallen and burned and after the shots were completed. With him were Larry Olivier and Vivien Leigh. Shhhhh: She's the Scarlett dark horse, and looks damned good. (Not for anybody's ears but your own: It's narrowed down to Paulette [Goddard], Jean Arthur, Joan Bennett, and Vivien Leigh."

TESTING, TESTING, TESTING

Selznick set up the testing schedule for the principal Scarlett candidates and told his staff, "Scarlett will definitely be decided upon as the result of this next group of tests."

Cukor worked with Jean Arthur, Joan Bennett, and Paulette Goddard, and on Wednesday, December 21 it was Vivien Leigh's turn. She had been rehearsing the three screen-test scenes and practicing her Southern accent every night for the past week with Olivier, but she was still nervous.

Before the camera, she displayed a fiery temperament in the lacing scene with Mammy before the barbecue. For the second test, the library scene with Ashley, she was a demanding, passionate Scarlett. In the third test, she fiercely tried to convince Ashley to run away with her to Mexico. Cukor was thrilled with the passion of her performances. Compared with the other candidates, he recalled, "There was an indescribable wildness about her."

Selznick spliced the tests together so that he could see all four actresses consecutively playing each scene. He viewed the scenes over and over again and then sent the film to Jock Whitney in New York for his reaction. Whitney deferred to his producer, and Selznick's decision was definite: Vivien Leigh would play Scarlett.

THE LONG-AWAITED ANNOUNCEMENT

Friday the thirteenth in January 1939 was a lucky day for Vivien Leigh: It was the day that Selznick announced her selection as Scarlett O'Hara. He softened the blow for the unlucky Scarlett contenders by sending each actress orchids and a personal note before the news was announced.

Selznick released the news first to Margaret Mitchell in three long Western Union telegrams that arrived in segments at fifteen-minute intervals. The first wire announced Vivien Leigh's casting as Scarlett, the second detailed the casting of Olivia de Havilland and Leslie Howard, and the third was a lengthy biographical sketch of Vivien Leigh. The bio skirted around Leigh's British nationality by mentioning her birth in India, her education in Europe and "her recent screen work in England." The release made no mention of Leigh's love, Laurence Olivier, nor their respective impending divorces.

Margaret Mitchell wanted her former colleagues at the *Constitution* to get this scoop of the year, so she ran back and forth between the telegraph office and the newspaper office carrying the pages of the wires as they arrived.

The newspaper, a morning edition, was about to go to press, so the editor tore out a portion of the front page. File clerks scurried around to find a photograph of Leigh, which was placed on the front page alongside the text of the wires as they were received and typeset.

But the clerks had a more difficult time locating a suitable photograph of Olivia de Havilland. According to Margaret Mitchell: "For a bad five minutes it looked as if a picture of Miss de Havilland in a scanty bathing suit was going to appear in the morning paper, bearing the caption 'Here is Melanie, a True Daughter of the Old South.' That picture was the only view of her the file clerk could find at first. I made loud lamentations at this, especially when the editor said, 'We can explain that Sherman's men had gotten away with the rest of her clothes.'" A more suitable

THE SCENE IN THE OFFICE OF DAVID SELZNICK
AFTER THE ANNOUNCEMENT OF THE CASTING OF VIVIEN
LEIGH AS SCARLETT O'HARA: SELZNICK, LEIGH,
HOWARD, DE HAVILLAND, AND DIRECTOR GEORGE CUKOR.

photograph was finally found, and Atlanta was the first to learn that *GWTW* had finally been cast.

TELEGRAMS TO MARGARET MITCHELL

After Selznick announced his cast on January 13, 1939, Vivien Leigh, Olivia de Havilland, and Leslie Howard sent telegrams to Margaret Mitchell. The telegrams were published in the Atlanta *Constitution* the following day.

From Vivien Leigh: "Dear Mrs. Marsh: If I can but feel that you are with me on this, the most important and trying task of my life, I pledge with all my heart I shall try to make Scarlett O'Hara live as you described her in your brilliant book. Warmest regards."

From Olivia de Havilland: "Dear Mrs. Marsh: The news that I am to play Melanie means a long-cherished dream realized. Now I hope for one thing more important, that is to play the role to your satisfaction."

From Leslie Howard: "Dear Mrs. Marsh: I am not at all envious of Rhett because thanks to you, it was Melanie, Ma'am, that I wanted. But seriously, I feel it a great honor to have been selected to enact one of the roles of your book, the title of which escapes me at the moment."

AMERICA'S REACTION

After the long-awaited announcement was officially released, the news was carried by almost every newspaper and radio station from coast to coast. A Gallup poll conducted afterward showed that 35% favored the selection of Vivien Leigh, 16% disapproved, 20% were undecided, and 29% hadn't heard the news.

One group who did hear the news was the Florida Daughters of the Confederacy, and they were not happy. They denounced Leigh's selection and threatened to boycott the film. Southern gentlemen sent outraged letters to newspapers stating their impassioned thoughts on the matter: "The selection of Vivien Leigh is a direct affront to the men who wore the Gray and an outrage to the memory of the heroes of 1776 who fought to free this land of British domination." Others wrote that an Englishwoman's portrayal of Scarlett was an "insult to Southern womanhood."

But the president-general of the United Daughters of the Confederacy saw the selection of Leigh in a different light: "I think Miss Leigh is an excellent solution of the problem, in which all the country has been keenly interested. . . . I have not been able to visualize any known American actress for portrayal of the part assigned to Miss Leigh. The character of Scarlett is interesting and thoroughly objectionable throughout. I do not consider her in any way whatever typical of Southern girls of the [18]60s."

LIGHTS!
CAMERA!
CHAOS!

◆

GEORGE CUKOR: DIRECTOR #1

In Hollywood, George Cukor was known as "a woman's director." He earned that reputation with his sensitive, insightful handling of women stars such as Katharine Hepburn, Greta Garbo, and Constance Bennett in such films as *A Bill of Divorcement*, *Camille*, and *What Price Hollywood?*.

It was only natural that Selznick select Cukor to direct *GWTW* shortly after Selznick bought the film rights. Selznick had long admired Cukor's work and felt that relating the story of Scarlett O'Hara needed Cukor's special touch.

From the beginning, Cukor was involved with every aspect of *GWTW*. He advised Selznick on the script; he traveled south to scout filming locations and to seek potential Scarlett candidates. Cukor coached and tested actors and actresses during the casting of the film; he worked with production designer William Cameron Menzies to prepare "a complete script in sketch form, showing actual camera setups, lighting, etc."

Cukor devoted two intense years to the preproduction work on *GWTW*. But only a brief two weeks after he had called "Action!" George Cukor found himself replaced as director of the film.

THE CONTINUING SAGA
OF TRANSFORMING
GWTW INTO A SCRIPT,
Part Two

The next writer that Selznick selected to work on Howard's *GWTW* script was well-known script fixer Jo Swerling. Swerling went with Selznick on a working vacation to Bermuda and threw himself into the project. After countless scene rewrites, however, Selznick was still not satisfied with the script.

When Selznick returned from Bermuda, he approached another writer, playwright Oliver H.P. Garrett. An accommodating fellow, Garrett agreed to accompany Selznick on his transcontinental train trip from New York to Los Angeles. As the Super-Chief thundered along to the West Coast, Garrett was in his stateroom hard at work revising the *GWTW* script.

What frustrated the writers who worked with Selznick was his insistence that the script contain Margaret Mitchell's dialogue. Selznick was convinced that no more than one hundred lines of new dialogue would be needed. For the writer, that meant endless hunting through the novel, searching for lines of dialogue to use in constructing a scene.

Garrett's tenure on the script was not long. He was soon replaced by yet another writer who was replaced by a succession of still other writers. Those tapped by Selznick included John Van Druten, Charles MacArthur, Winston Miller, John Balderstron, Michael Foster, and Edwin Justus Mayer. F. Scott Fitzgerald even had a crack at the script.

Fitzgerald's career was on the downslide when he undertook rewriting the *GWTW* script in January 1939. His contract to write for MGM was not being renewed, so during the remaining weeks, the studio lent him to Selznick to rewrite dialogue. He edited the script mercilessly, cutting paragraphs of flowery dialogue that he described as "trite and stagy." But about halfway through his blue-pencilling of the script, a snag developed. Selznick was concerned that the character of Aunt Pittypat was not funny enough. Through an all-night conference with Selznick and director Cukor, Fitzgerald struggled to find more amusing lines for the character. But his suggestions bombed, and he was sent home. Selznick fired him the next day.

As a result, on the day before the start of the principal shooting, Selznick still didn't have a complete script. Dauntless, he assured Jock Whitney: "Don't get panicky at the seemingly small amount of final revised script. . . . It is so clearly in my mind that I can tell you the picture from beginning to end, almost shot for shot."

What Selznick did have was the novel, the Sidney Howard script, and the Howard-Garrett script. He believed that the Garrett script was superior in its continuity and basic storytelling but not as good as the Howard script in the crafting of individual scenes. "The job that remains to be done is to telescope the three into the shortest possible form," Selznick told Whitney. And Selznick believed he could do that himself. (*To be continued . . .*)

MELANIE'S LABOR PAINS

"Melanie's pains were harder now. Her long hair was drenched in sweat and her gown stuck in wet spots to her body." Olivia de Havilland wanted to portray the scene of Melanie's giving birth as realistically as Margaret Mitchell had written it.

Since childbirth was a foreign experience for her, she prepared for the scene by visiting the Los Angeles County Hospital. There, dressed as a nurse, she observed births in the delivery room. After watching and listening, she noticed that labor pains were not continuous; they came in waves.

She reported this to Cukor as they rehearsed Melanie's labor scene. When filming began, Cukor became inspired. He grabbed and sharply twisted de Havilland's ankle under the blankets whenever he wanted her to simulate a new cycle of pain.

FIRED!

The filming of *GWTW* was progressing as slowly as molasses in January 1939. Because of difficulties with the script, Cukor had to shoot out of sequence. In the two weeks that followed the beginning of principal filming, Cukor had directed the opening scene of Scarlett and the Tarletons on Tara's porch, the birth of Melanie's baby, Scarlett's shooting of the Yankee deserter, and Rhett's presenting the Paris hat to Scarlett. Cukor was working on the scenes from the Atlanta Bazaar when Selznick fired him.

Things went sour quickly for a number of reasons. The script was the main problem. Changes in scenes and dialogue arrived almost daily on the set. Out of necessity, Cukor substituted dialogue from the novel for the often-unplayable lines of the still-unfinished script. He even rewrote scenes before he shot them to make them more realistic. This not only caused delays in the shooting schedule but incurred Selznick's wrath as well.

After Selznick viewed the rushes, he and Cukor met head-on in heated confrontations. Selznick resented anyone tampering with his masterpiece. He told Cukor he expected to see each scene rehearsed before it was filmed to "avoid projection-room surprises for me." Selznick was concerned that Cukor, in his zeal for capturing the nuances of characters and scenes, was forsaking the panoramic sweep of the film. Selznick then began visiting the set, offering his unasked-for opinions, and driving the director to distraction with his interference.

Clark Gable, too, was becoming dissatisfied with Cukor. He was convinced that the "woman's director" was ignoring him and throwing the film toward its female stars. Gable and Cukor clashed over Rhett's Southern accent. Cukor argued for a more distinctive accent, but Gable resisted and convinced Selznick to back him. Gable also hated the slow pace at which filming was taking place. His view was echoed by Leslie Howard, who wrote to his daughter: "After seven days' shooting they are five days behind schedule."

On February 13 Selznick and Cukor issued a joint statement: "As a result of a series of disagreements between us over many of the individual scenes of *Gone With the Wind*, we have mutually decided that the only solution is for a new director to be selected at as early a date as is practicable." Cukor was out, and production shut down for two weeks.

When Vivien Leigh and Olivia de Havilland heard that Cukor had been fired, they were rehearsing a scene from the Atlanta Bazaar sequence. In their black mourning costumes, they stormed into Selznick's office and pleaded for nearly an hour that Cukor be reinstated. Cukor had been the craftsman who had shaped their roles, they implored. Without his guidance, they would be lost. But Selznick would not reconsider. Vivien even threatened to walk off the film until she was warned about the legal ramifications of breaking a contract.

The stars returned to work, but they were distraught. Leigh later wrote to her husband Leigh Holman that Cukor "was my last hope of ever enjoying the film."

Cukor's influence did not end with his firing, though. When Vivien Leigh felt she needed help in understanding an upcoming scene, she secretly met Cukor for direction after regular studio hours. Olivia de Havilland also saw Cukor on the qt. She met him on Sundays or dined with him when she needed help with development of her character. But neither actress let on to the other what she was doing.

De Havilland, perhaps feeling guilty, questioned Cukor about the propriety of working with him behind Leigh's back. Cukor replied that he didn't see anything wrong with it since Leigh was doing the same thing. Cukor essentially ghost-directed their performances in this way until the end of filming.

VICTOR FLEMING: DIRECTOR #2

To replace Cukor, Selznick approached MGM contract director Victor Fleming. Fleming was not interested in taking over the directorial reins of the troubled *GWTW*. At the time, he was manic with Munchkins on the set of *The Wizard of Oz* and didn't want to take on another exhausting project.

Gable was all for Fleming. Fleming had a reputation of being a "man's director" and had directed Gable in *Test Pilot* and *Red Dust*. The two were also old friends and enjoyed motorcycling, carousing, and drinking together. Gable appealed to Fleming to accept the job on the basis of their friendship. MGM was applying pressure as well, and Fleming reluctantly agreed to take on the project.

Fleming met with Selznick to view the film footage of *GWTW* that had been shot so far. Fleming was never a man to pull any punches. As soon as the lights came up in the projection room, he turned to Selznick and said, "David, your f—ing script is no f—ing good."

UPI/BETTMAN ARCHIVE

NEWLY HIRED DIRECTOR VICTOR FLEMING
WITH HOWARD AND LEIGH.

THE CONTINUING SAGA OF TRANSFORMING *GWTW* INTO A SCRIPT, Part Three

Once production was underway, Selznick assumed the enormous task of writing the script for *GWTW*. He stayed awake night after night writing and rewriting the scenes that would be shot the following day. Cukor's complaints about the script escalated. Something had to give, and that something proved to be George Cukor.

Since Sidney Howard's original effort, the script had been changed by numerous pens. Selznick had resorted to printing revised pages on different shades of colored paper in an effort to keep track of each writer's contributions. By the time Victor Fleming took over directorial duties, the script resembled a veritable rainbow. Fleming's graphic estimation of the script's quality shocked Selznick into admitting that the script was, indeed, in serious trouble.

Selznick had no time to lose in reviving his script. Each day of suspended filming was costing the studio over $65,000. So Selznick turned to a famous scrip doctor who had a reputation for working miracles, Ben Hecht.

Hecht, brilliant but cynical, had begun his career as a playwright with his partner Charles MacArthur. Together they penned *The Front Page* and *Twentieth Century*. Lured by more lucrative work in Hollywood, Hecht then turned to writing scripts. He wrote *Design for Living* for Ernst Lubitsch and *Notorious* for Alfred Hitchcock. He always worked for the best price because he was a shrewd bargainer and a fast writer. He had written *Nothing Sacred* for Selznick in two weeks and rewrote *Hurricane* for Samuel Goldwyn in two days.

Selznick and Fleming arrived at Hecht's house early on Sunday morning. They spirited Hecht away in Selznick's car, and on the way to the studio they came to terms: Selznick would pay Hecht $15,000 for one week's work.

At the studio, Selznick was horrified to learn that Hecht had never read *Gone With the Wind*. Fleming admitted that he had not either so Selznick launched into an oral synopsis that took over an hour. "I had seldom heard a more involved plot," Hecht remembered. "My verdict was that nobody could make a sensible movie out of it."

Hecht read the existing script, a real "humpty-dumpty job." He then asked Selznick if any one of the previous writers had produced a better version. Selznick suddenly remembered Sidney Howard's two-year-old draft and sent secretaries scurrying to find it. Hecht called it a "superb treatment" that needed only substantial editing and agreed to base his rewrite on Howard's script.

In Selznick's office for the next five days and nights Hecht attacked the script mercilessly in 18- to 24-hour stretches. Since he was not familiar with the characters, Selznick and Fleming acted out each scene as Hecht edited.

The pace was arduous and took its toll. Selznick ruled that food interfered with creativity so he banned all sustenance except for bananas and salted peanuts. Selznick took Benzedrine to keep awake and recommended the wonder drug to his cohorts. On day four, Fleming suffered a burst blood vessel in his eye, and the following day, Selznick collapsed while eating a banana. Nevertheless, at the end of the week, Hecht had succeeded in revising the entire first half of the script. (*To be continued . . .*)

THE CONTINUING SAGA OF TRANSFORMING *GWTW* INTO A SCRIPT, Part Four

Selznick tried to convince Ben Hecht to stay and finish the second part of the script. Hecht felt "there wasn't enough money in the world for this kind of suicidal work—eighteen to twenty hours a day—and I got out in a hurry."

With Hecht gone, Selznick decided to undertake the rewriting of Part Two on his own. By April, though, he was hopelessly behind in the rewriting, and the filming was floundering under the awful dialogue. In desperation, he sent out an SOS to the original architect of the script, Sidney Howard.

Howard agreed to work on the script for one week and during that time rewrote several major scenes in the second part. He fought with Selznick over the producer's desire to have a large church wedding for Scarlett's marriage to Frank Kennedy and over other issues. Howard tackled the final scene in which Rhett leaves Scarlett and felt his work was done. He was sure, however, that Selznick would rewrite the rewrite, then call him back again to salvage the script. Selznick did attack the script again, but Howard never worked again on it.

TRAGEDY STRIKES SIDNEY HOWARD

Sidney Howard owned a seven hundred-acre cattle farm in Tyringham, Massachusetts. One day in August 1939 he was attempting to start a tractor in his shed. What he didn't know was that the tractor had been left in gear. He cranked the handle in front of the tractor, the engine engaged, and the tractor leaped forward. Howard was crushed to death against a wall.

COACHES ON THE SET

Selznick recruited special advisors to work on *GWTW*. The following were among them:

Will Price

A Southern dialogue director, Will Price was charged with coaching the actors in Southern dialects. He worked with acting candidates to prepare them for their auditions, and during filming he coached the stars and the bit players.

Susan Myrick

She was a newspaperwoman with the *Macon Telegraph* and a friend of Margaret Mitchell's. Margaret recommended her to Kay Brown as an expert on Southern speech, manners, and customs. For example, she pointed out to Selznick, but was overruled, that it would be inappropriate for Scarlett to wear a long-veiled street bonnet at the evening Bazaar. She was more successful in convincing him that it would be an insult for Rhett to use Belle Watling's carriage when calling on Scarlett. Myrick's work on the film earned her the title of "The Emily Post of the South."

Wilbur Kuritz

This noted Civil War historian, artist, and architect also was recommended by Margaret Mitchell. She had sought his expertise when checking the accuracy of two chapters of her novel. He worked closely with William Cameron Menzies and provided sketches of the city of Atlanta, common household items, and farm implements. He was the authority on endless historical details: the cropping of horses' tails, the use of oral thermometers, the construction of a well, the design of tombstones. His thirty-two-page description of a typical pre–Civil War Southern barbecue was invaluable during the planning and execution of the set for the Wilkes's barbecue.

TURNER ENTERTAINMENT

A SEAMSTRESS AT WORK ON A *GWTW* COSTUME.

HORSING AROUND WITH THOMAS MITCHELL

When Thomas Mitchell agreed to portray Scarlett's father, he argued for a special clause in his contract. Mitchell had a long-standing fear of horses, and the clause stipulated that he would not have to ride. But director Victor Fleming may have had other ideas in mind.

Fleming coaxed a protesting Mitchell into the saddle of his horse, the famous Silver of the Lone Ranger movie serial. The expressed intention was to shoot stationary close-ups. Fleming pointed out to the agitated actor that stagehands off to the side were holding the horse with wires attached to the bridle.

Mitchell, his face ruddy and his eyes wide with fear, settled uneasily into the saddle. Suddenly, spooked either by Mitchell's nervousness or an unseen instigator, the horse bolted. With a terrified Mitchell gripping the reins, the horse galloped at top speed across the open fields. And Fleming, by design or coincidence, managed to capture the entire episode on film.

LOVE AMONG THE STARS

• Clark Gable's romance with Carole Lombard, although he was still married to Ria Langham Gable, sizzled during the filming of *GWTW*. The pair married in March 1939 when Gable had a break from shooting.

• The love affair between Vivien Leigh and Laurence Olivier was hotter than the flames that swept through the streets of Atlanta. Leigh was married to London barrister Leigh Holman, and Olivier was married to actress Jill Esmond. Each marriage was blessed with a young child. The lovers were planning to marry as soon as their divorces could be arranged but until then were living together in a Beverly Hills house. Selznick, ever afraid of scandal, appealed to his brother Myron to get Olivier out of town. As a result, after the filming of *Wuthering Heights* ended in April 1939, Olivier departed for a role in the Broadway play *No Time for Comedy*.

• Like Olivier, Leslie Howard was a married man with a family. And Howard was also madly in love and living with a woman who was not his wife. Attractive, red-haired Violette Cunningham was Howard's production assistant, but most people guessed that theirs was a deeper relationship. Unlike Olivier, who was barred from the *GWTW* set, Cunningham accompanied Howard to the set every day.

• Olivia de Havilland was single and dating millionaire aviator Howard Hughes. When he proposed marriage during the filming of *GWTW*, Hughes made it clear he wanted to wait until he turned fifty— in seventeen years—to tie the knot. But Hughes wanted de Havilland to give up her career then and there and devote her life to him. She refused his offer, but they continued to see each other. Their relationship finally ended in June 1939 when, at a party, Hughes spontaneously proposed to de Havilland's sister, Joan Fontaine.

A WHO'S WHO OF
SELZNICK'S PRODUCTION TEAM

Edward G. Boyle - Interior Decoration
Ridgeway Callow - Assistant Director
Wilfrid M. Cline - Technicolor Associate
Jack Cosgrove - Special Photographic Effects
Lillian K. Deighton - Research
Connie Earle - Production Continuity
Reeves Eason - Second Unit Director
Frank Floyd - Dance Director
James Forney - Drapes
John Frederics - Scarlett's Hats
Ernest Haller - Photography
Natalie Kalmus - Technicolor Company Supervision
Barbara Keon - Scenario Assistant
Hal C. Kern - Supervising Film Editor
Raymond Klune - Production Manager
Edward Lambert - Wardrobe
Frank Maher - Sound Recorder
William Cameron Menzies - Production Designer
James E. Newcom - Associate Film Editor
Ben Nye - Makeup
Joseph B. Platt - Interiors
Walter Plunkett - Costumes
Eddie Prinz - Dance Director
Ray Rennahan - Technicolor Associate
Hazel Rogers - Hair Stylist
Lydia Schiller - Production Continuity
Eddie Schmidt - Rhett's Wardrobe
Eric Stacey - Assistant Director
Max Steiner - Music
Monty Westmore - Makeup and Hairstyling
Lyle Wheeler - Art Director
Florence Yoch - Tara's Landscaper
Lee Zavitz - Fire Effects

COSTUMES

The Man Who Had Designs on Scarlett

Scarlett's exquisite costumes were designed by Walter Plunkett, a contract designer borrowed from Metro-Goldwyn-Mayer.

He started out at RKO in 1926 and first worked with Selznick in 1937's *Nothing Sacred*. In 1946 Plunkett began a twenty-year association with MGM. There his work earned him kudos as a designer of historical costumes.

After Selznick selected him to design the costumes for *GWTW*, Plunkett traveled to Atlanta to research the styles of clothing worn during the Civil War and Reconstruction periods. He also collected fabric swatches from dresses displayed in Southern museums. These swatches were sent to a Pennsylvania textile mill, which made all the cotton cloth used for the costumes.

When he returned to Selznick's studio, Plunkett was faced with designing gowns and petticoats for an unknown actress, since the role of Scarlett had not yet been cast. Additionally, Plunkett supervised the Civil War fashions industry that had sprung up on the studio lot. Seamstresses, weavers, hatmakers, and shoemakers created hundreds of dresses, uniforms, and accessories. A retired corset maker provided expertise on antebellum foundation garments, and ironworkers forged hoops for skirts.

Plunkett's matchless *GWTW* designs would be unrecognized by an Academy Award since the category of Best Costume Design did not exist at the time. But in 1951 he and two other designers shared the Academy Award for their work on *An American in Paris*. Plunkett's costumes earned him Oscar nominations for *The Magnificent Yankee, That Forsyte Woman, Kind Lady, The Actress, Young Bess, Raintree County, Some Came Running, Pocketful of Miracles,* and *How the West Was Won*.

Gable's Wardrobe Didn't Suit Him

Gable not only had problems with *GWTW*'s script and director Cukor; he was also unhappy with the wardrobe made for him by Selznick's costume department. The shirt collars choked him, and the suits and cravats were ill fitting.

He complained to Selznick, who fired off a memo to the wardrobe department: "I think it is very disappointing indeed to have the elegant Rhett Butler wandering around with clothes that look as though he had bought them at the Hart, Schaffner, and Marx of that period and walked right out of the store with them." Selznick urged his wardrobe staff to observe Gable's personal wardrobe: "Look at how well he looks in his own clothes generally, and compare the fit and the tailoring and the general attractiveness with what I regard as the awful costuming job we are doing with him."

To keep his star happy, Selznick ordered a complete new wardrobe made for Rhett Butler by Gable's Beverly Hills tailor, Eddie Schmidt.

Other Design Notes

• Plunkett fashioned 5,500 wardrobe items for *GWTW* at a cost of $153,818. The women's costumes alone totaled $98,154. The cost for laundering the costumes during production was $10,000.

• Selznick insisted on complete authenticity in the costumes. For instance, he directed Plunkett to use expensive lace to make petticoats for the ladies. Ann Rutherford, playing Scarlett's sister Carreen, voiced her opinion that the cost was extravagant especially since the audience would not know the lace was there. "But you'll know it's there," was Selznick's reply.

• Scarlett wears a calico dress in various stages of disintegration longer than any other costume in the film. The calico first appears in the Shadow sequence in the Atlanta Hospital and is seen for the last time when Scarlett tears down her mother's portieres to make the green velvet drapery dress. The calico was accessorized with bonnets, shawls, and aprons in various scenes.

Actually, twenty-seven copies of the dress were made for Leigh and her stand-ins. Some were used in their original condition for the earlier scenes; others had to be aged for subsequent ones. In the aging process, the calicoes were subjected to rubbings with sandpaper and washings in a solution of water, bleach, and sand. A special dye was added to the wash water when a dingy look was needed. For the later scenes, the calico dress was constructed using the reverse side of the material.

• Probably the most famous costume in movie history is the drapery dress that Scarlett wears to Atlanta. She has to go "looking like a queen" to convince Rhett to give her the tax money for Tara, and the gown symbolizes her firm determination to survive.

• Director Fleming demanded a good deal of cleavage for Leigh's appearance in the décolleté burgundy velvet gown Scarlett wears to

THE KOBAL COLLECTION/MGM

SCARLETT IN HER CALICO DRESS.

Ashley's birthday party. "For Christ's sake, let's get a good look at the girl's boobs," he told Walter Plunkett. Because Leigh's breasts spread sideways naturally, Plunkett had to tape them tightly together. The taping forced her breasts forward and upward, which resulted in the desired deep cleavage.

TURMOIL ON THE SET

Filming resumed on March 1 with Victor Fleming at the directorial helm. At his first meeting with assistant directors Eric Stacey and Ridgeway Callow, Fleming left no doubt about how he would run things. "So you're the famous Selznick team," Fleming barked. "By the time we finish this picture, you're both going to have a nervous breakdown." Fleming browbeat and drove his cast and crew mercilessly. In just a few days, he was thoroughly disliked by almost everyone on the set.

Gable was happy to have Fleming on board. At last he could feel comfortable in the hands of a director who understood him. Gable relaxed on the set, had lunch with the crew, and joined in their jokes.

Vivien Leigh, on the other hand, was bitter about Cukor's replacement especially after Fleming declared, "I'm going to make this picture a melodrama." In an attempt to win her over, Fleming nicknamed Leigh "Fiddle-dee-dee," but this just increased her resentment toward him. Adding to her misery was the fact that Olivier had gone to New York. In great despair, Leigh wrote to her husband, "It is really very miserable, and going terribly slowly." A few days later she wrote, "I was a *fool* to have done it." Now the only goal for Leigh was to complete the picture as soon as possible and be reunited with Olivier. To that end she pushed herself by working sixteen-hour days, six days a week.

Leigh's exhaustion and frayed nerves were not helped by Selznick's rewritten script pages, which appeared on the set daily. The shooting was not done in sequence so Leigh was frequently called upon to switch from a flirtatious Scarlett in one scene to a grieving Scarlett in the very next.

Leigh constantly complained about Selznick's unplayable dialogue and kept a copy of Margaret Mitchell's novel with her to bolster her arguments. Selznick frequently yelled at her to "please put that damn book away."

One dialogue battle that Leigh went head-to-head with Selznick on concerned Scarlett's line when Rhett visits after Frank Kennedy's funeral. A tipsy Scarlett tearfully admits to Rhett that she is glad her mother is dead and can't see her. "She brought me up to be so kind and thoughtful, just like her, and I've turned out to be such a disappointment." Selznick kept cutting the line, but Leigh fought for it. She believed it defined Scarlett's character. Leigh won, and the line stayed in.

Fleming also was no help to Leigh when it came to development of her character since he was more used to working with men in action films. When she would ask how a particular scene should be played, Fleming would reply, "Ham it up."

Leigh also resented Fleming's attempt to portray Scarlett as a totally bitchy woman with no motivating factors. The veneer of professionalism that had characterized their working relationship quickly deteriorated. Quarrels erupted and frequently ended with Leigh in tears and Fleming enraged.

Things finally came to a head one morning when Leigh and Fleming were rehearsing the scene in which Scarlett finally rejects Rhett. "I can't do it, I simply can't do it," Leigh wailed. "This woman is nothing but a terrible bitch." Fleming, apparently at the end of his rope, rolled up his script and with fury in his eyes screamed, "Miss Leigh, you can stick this script up your royal British ass." Then he threw the script at her feet and walked off the set.

ENDLESS TROUBLE FOR *GWTW*

◆

Fleming was off the set. Leigh was exhausted from overwork. Gable felt railroaded into playing Rhett Butler. Leslie Howard saw the promise of directorial duties on *Intermezzo* fading in front of his eyes. Olivia de Havilland felt depressed without Cukor's guidance on the set. And the main cause of everyone's misery was David O. Selznick.

Selznick had an overwhelming feeling that *GWTW* was destined to be more than an epic: It would be a masterpiece. His masterpiece. To ensure this, he pushed himself beyond his own perfectionism by trying to control everything.

He personally approved every facet of production from the sets to the hairstyles and sometimes pushed Fleming aside to take over the direction of the film. At night when he should have been sleeping, he was writing the script, viewing the rushes of the day's filming, or gambling for hours at The Clover Club. To stay awake he took Benzedrine; to fall asleep he resorted to sleeping pills. His drive took its toll not only on himself but also on his staff, cast, and crew, who viewed him as even more argumentative and tyrannical than ever.

The relentless pace resulted in endless delays. Production costs skyrocketed, and Selznick was forced to seek further financing from his backers. Then he began to doubt the results of his work. He complained that the costumes looked too new, that Tara's fields looked like "the back yard of a suburban home," and that the Southern accents of the actors were not convincing. The filming of *GWTW* was in serious trouble.

AN APPEAL TO FLEMING

Fleming didn't appear at the studio for the next two days and refused to answer the telephone. Finally Selznick, Gable, and Leigh drove to his house bearing a cage of lovebirds as a peace offering. Peace was established. Then Selznick asked Fleming to return to the set, even offering him a share of the profits. "What do you think I am, a chump?" Fleming replied. "This picture is going to be the biggest white elephant in history." Reluctantly, Fleming agreed to return to work.

But working under intense pressure once again just made Fleming more irritable. Explosions on the set were more commonplace than before. On April 26, an overwrought Fleming again walked off the set, threatening to drive his car off the nearest cliff. He claimed he had suffered a nervous breakdown.

Once again production ground to a halt while Selznick searched for yet another director for *GWTW*.

DIRECTOR #3

To replace Victor Fleming, Selznick chose MGM contract director Sam Wood, who had just finished filming *Goodbye, Mr. Chips*. Wood had worked as an assistant director with Cecil B. DeMille, the master of the movie spectacular. While at Paramount Pictures, Wood directed films starring Wallace Reid, Gloria Swanson, and Rudolph Valentino. His recent work for MGM included the Marx Brothers movies *A Night at the Opera* and *A Day at the Races*.

Wood began directing *GWTW* on May 1 and started his schedule with the scenes of Scarlett and Ashley embracing at the lumber mill and Belle Watling approaching Melanie on the hospital steps. To make up for lost time, he worked at a brisk pace for the next two weeks.

Wood was not a director with a great deal of imagination. But at this point, Selznick was not looking for a creator. He was looking for a channel for his own ideas, and Wood filled the bill.

To the surprise of cast and crew who were just getting used to Wood's style, a recuperated Victor Fleming returned to the set on May 15. Selznick decided to retain Wood to maintain the filming pace and to take some of the pressure off Fleming.

Wood directed sequences such as Scarlett giving Gerald's watch to

Pork and Scarlett tearing down the draperies, while Fleming directed Gable's scenes. The stars frequently found themselves working with Fleming in the morning and Wood in the afternoon. Others contributing to the directorial duties were William Cameron Menzies, who directed a second camera unit, and Eric Stacey and Reeves Eason, who filmed incidental shots.

GWTW'S JINXED SCENES

Scarlett and the Tarletons on Tara's Porch

On Thursday, January 26, 1939, George Cukor yelled "Action," and the principal photography began. Vivien Leigh in her green- sprig muslin dress warned the Tarleton boys that one more mention of war would send her right into the house. But when the rushes of that scene were shown, Selznick was aghast that the Tarletons' curly hairstyles had photographed bright orange. He ordered the scene reshot.

Four days later, the trio once more appeared on Tara's porch. This time the Tarletons' hairstyles were straightened and darkened. Selznick was pleased with the results of their coiffures, but their acting abilities left much to be desired.

When Victor Fleming took over directing duties on March 1, the porch scene was shot again. This third time the camera caught Scarlett's flirtations from a different angle, but this was no better than the previous two tries.

On June 14 Vivien Leigh reported for the scene of Gerald's walk with Scarlett in which he declares that "land's the only thing that lasts." While preparing for that scene, she learned that Selznick had decided she would wear the white, high-necked, ruffled dress from the Evening Prayers sequence. White, Selznick believed, would make Scarlett look more virginal. That meant, of course, that all of the previously filmed porch scenes had to be scrapped. Not even close-ups could be saved.

The fourth version of the porch scene was filmed on Monday, June 26. Vivien Leigh, dressed in white, listened as the Tarletons told her that Ashley was engaged to marry his cousin Melanie. But Leigh's face reflected more than distress at this news. She looked pale, haggard, and worn from five months of grueling work.

On October 13, Victor Fleming directed the fifth version of the porch scene. Leigh, fresh from a vacation, was well rested and once again the beautiful image of sixteen-year-old Scarlett as she complained to the Tarletons that talk of war was spoiling all the fun at every party.

Belle Watling Waiting for Melanie Outside the Hospital

During the first week of May, Sam Wood directed the scene of Belle Watling waiting for Melanie outside the hospital. Ona Munson's costume was heavily padded to make her look well-endowed. But the costume department outdid themselves, and Wood decided that the prominence of Belle's bosom would not be approved by the censors in the Hays Office. He reshot the scené the following week, but this was equally unsatisfactory.

Victor Fleming took a crack at directing this scene on Friday, June 2. During the shooting, Munson's bosom was rendered more discreetly, and the scene was successful.

The Arrival of Ellen

George Cukor directed Ellen O'Hara's return to Tara on Saturday, January 28. Barbara O'Neil as Ellen informed Robert Gleckler, who was playing Jonas Wilkerson, that she had just come from Emmy Slattery's bedside. Cukor and Selznick were both pleased with that scene as well as others Gleckler had done.

But tragedy struck during a break in production. Gleckler died of uremic poisoning on February 25. Victor Jory was hired to replace Gleckler, and all of the previously filmed scenes were reshot under the direction of Victor Fleming.

SELZNICK'S FOLLY

Delays, friction, and dismissals during the filming of *GWTW* caused consternation among Selznick's backers. Production overhead was soaring, and they were beginning to think they would never see a return on their investment. Even those in the movie industry began having second thoughts about Selznick's "folly." Soon the shoptalk around Hollywood buzzed that *GWTW* was going to be a disaster.

Film insiders gossiped about Selznick, made him the butt of their jokes, and predicted his financial ruin. Cecil B. DeMille tweaked Selznick's nose by announcing a nationwide search to find a cigar-store Indian for a scene in his film *Union Pacific*. Even Sid Grauman, who owned the Chinese Movie Theater, added his two cents. At a large dinner party, he unveiled a life-size wax statue of a very old David Selznick leaning on a cane. A placard at the base of the statue proclaimed: "Selznick after the final shot of *Gone With the Wind*."

Outsiders hurled epithets such as "bust," "white elephant," and "turkey" in *GWTW*'s direction. But this abuse had the very opposite reaction. It only intensified Selznick's determination that *GWTW* would be the greatest picture ever made.

FUN ON THE SET

To break the tension of the long workdays, stagehands and actors occasionally played jokes on one another. Here are some samples:

• Stagehands placed percussive caps beneath the boards of sets under construction. When a workman nailing the boards struck them with a hammer, the caps exploded. The crew in on the gag then burst into screams of "The Yankees is coming!"

• As a prank on Clark Gable, stagehands sewed seventy pounds of lead weights into the skirt of Olivia de Havilland's costume. For the scene of Rhett's rescue, Gable had to lift a weakened Melanie from her bed and carry her down the stairs to the wagon that would whisk them out of Atlanta. Gable, staggering under the added weight, good-naturedly asked if the crew had nailed de Havilland to the floor.

• Gable turned the tables on Hattie McDaniel during the filming of "Rhett Pours Mammy a Drink." After the birth of his daughter Bonnie, Rhett celebrates by offering Mammy a glass of sherry.

Cold tea is the traditional liquor substitute used on movie sets. Gable poured from the decanter while McDaniel delivered her line then downed her drink. An instant later, she froze. Tears came to her reddened eyes, and cast and crew roared with laughter. Gable had put real scotch in the decanter in place of the cold tea.

• The joke was on the crew during the filming of "Scarlett Killing the Yankee Deserter." After Scarlett shoots the deserter, she tells Melanie to take off her nightgown so she can wrap it around the soldier's head. Word had spread like wildfire throughout the studio that de Havilland wore nothing underneath the nightgown. On the day of the filming, a large crowd of studio workers gathered behind the lights to watch the scene. As de Havilland slipped off the nightgown, the hopes of the crowd were dashed. There she was without her nightgown, but she wore a blouse and had on a pair of slacks that were rolled up to her knees.

To while away the time between takes, Gable and Leigh retreated to a corner of the set to play games. He taught her the fundamentals of backgammon, and she taught him Battleship, a naval war game of

UPI/BETTMAN ARCHIVE

GABLE AND LEIGH PLAYING CHINESE CHECKERS BETWEEN TAKES.

skill and strategy. Time after time, Leigh soundly trounced Gable at both games.

THE FAMOUS CRANE SHOT

Scarlett searching for Dr. Meade at the train depot is one of the most memorable scenes in *GWTW*. Known as the crane shot, the scene begins with Scarlett's arrival at the depot. She walks gingerly among the "hundreds of wounded men . . . stretched out in endless rows." When she finds Dr. Meade, she tells him that Melanie is having her baby, and Meade is incredulous. "Are you crazy? I can't leave these men for a baby! They're dying—hundreds of them." To underscore his words, the camera slowly pulls back and up to show a field of "stinking, bleeding bodies broiling under the glaring sun" and comes to rest on the tattered Confederate flag flapping in the wind.

The planning of this scene started four months before it was filmed. The major problem was getting the camera up to the required height. The camera crew estimated that by the end of the scene, the camera needed to be ninety feet off the ground. But the tallest camera crane available in Hollywood only reached a height of twenty-five feet.

Selznick's production manager, Ray Klune, contacted a southern California construction company that owned a crane with an extension range of 125 feet. He rented the crane, which was mounted on a truck for ten days. During tests, he found that vibrations from the truck's engine shook the camera at the beginning and end of the scene. To solve the problem, Klune ordered the building of a 150-foot-long concrete ramp. The truck slid smoothly down the ramp while the arm of the crane lifted the camera easily into the air to capture the breathtaking panorama.

In addition to the technical problems of the crane shot, Selznick was faced with populating the scene. The day before filming, he ordered 2,500 extras from Central Casting. But on such short notice, Casting could only provide 1,500. Selznick decided to use them and to intersperse 1,000 dummies among the live actors. The extras were instructed to rock the dummies to simulate animation.

Later, the Screen Extras Guild tried to extract union dues from Selznick for the dummies as well as the live extras. Selznick balked and challenged the Guild to come up with 2,500 extras. They couldn't do it, and they dropped their claim.

WHAT DID YOU DO ON YOUR DAY OFF, CLARK?

In early March, Ria Gable's divorce came through. Clark Gable was now free to marry Carole Lombard. On the day the news of the divorce broke, Hearst newspaper columnist Louella Parsons asked Lombard about the pair's wedding plans. Lombard told her, "When Clark gets a few days off, perhaps we'll sneak away and have the ceremony performed."

On March 28, Gable learned that because of changes in the shooting schedule, he would have two days off from his work on *GWTW*. The pair were overjoyed and quickly and quietly made plans for their elopement.

They did not want to alert the press, especially the reporters who had been haunting Lombard's Bel-Air house, hoping to scoop the wedding of the year. But luck was with the lovers. The entire corps of reporters was being sent on a junket to San Francisco to cover the world premiere of *The Story of Alexander Graham Bell*. It was a perfect opportunity for Gable and Lombard to slip away and be married.

Hollywood's golden couple had a nickel-plated elopement. They packed their wedding clothes in a suitcase and dressed in ragtag shirts and scruffy dungarees. For further camouflage, Lombard wore no makeup and tied her blonde hair in pigtails. The pair, accompanied by MGM's publicity man Otto Winkler, took off at 4:30 in the morning on March 29 in Winkler's blue DeSoto coupe and headed for Kingman, Arizona, 357 miles away.

Along the way, the trio munched on sandwiches and drank thermos bottles of coffee. Gable and Winkler shared the driving, and during stops for gas, Gable hid in the rumble seat to avoid recognition. One of the last stops before reaching Kingman was to buy wedding flowers: a corsage of pink roses and lilies of the valley for the bride and carnation boutonnieres for the groom and best man Winkler. Total cost: fifty cents.

At 4:00 that afternoon in Kingman's town hall, Gable and Lombard completed the necessary marriage forms, then hurried to the rectory of the First Methodist-Episcopal Church. There they changed into their wedding clothes and met the minister and his wife. The quiet ceremony then began.

Gable, wearing a blue serge suit, a white shirt, and a patterned tie, nervously placed a platinum band on his bride's finger. Dressed in a tailored, light gray, flannel suit, Lombard shed tears of joy.

After the ceremony, the newlyweds, with Winkler driving, headed back to Los Angeles. Along the way they phoned the news of their marriage to MGM and wired Louella Parsons and her boss, William Randolph Hearst.

The new Mr. and Mrs. Clark Gable arrived at Lombard's house nearly twenty-four hours after they had left. They had only a few hours to rest up before facing reporters during a press conference scheduled for later that morning. And the most popular tongue-in-cheek question surely would be, What did you do on your day off, Clark?

LESLIE HOWARD: FOILED AGAIN

"I hate the damn part," Leslie Howard complained in a letter to his daughter. "I'm not nearly beautiful or young enough for Ashley, and it makes me sick being fixed up to look attractive."

Howard's initial disinterest in playing Ashley eventually grew to resentment. He frequently arrived late on the set despite lectures from Selznick. He was unprepared and ruined takes when he flubbed his lines. His feelings about the film were summed up as "a terrible lot of nonsense—heaven help me if I ever read the book."

He never did. Right before filming the paddock scene, Selznick sent a pointed memo to Howard. "I send you herewith a copy of that book you ought to get around to reading some time, called *Gone with the Wind*. I think the book has a great future and might make a very good picture." Selznick reminded Howard of his promise to read that part of the book that contained the paddock scene to get a better understanding of Ashley. If at all, Howard probably read those ten pages and no more.

Howard's mind was on *Intermezzo*, the plum that Selznick had used to snare him into the role of Ashley. Howard would have the role of the married violinist who falls in love with his accompanist, played by the new Swedish star Ingrid Bergman.

Unfortunately, delays in filming *GWTW* caused its shooting schedule to overlap with the production start of *Intermezzo*. Howard soon found himself racing from the set of one film to that of the other. Playing two roles simultaneously left Howard precious little time to undertake the production duties promised by Selznick. And tragically, *Intermezzo* would be Leslie Howard's last film.

CARE FOR ANOTHER RADISH, MISS LEIGH?

At the stirring conclusion of Part One, an exhausted Scarlett trudges into Tara's backyard and views the Yankee devastation. Seized by hunger she falls to her knees, and her hand plucks a radish from the garden. She tries to eat the pungent vegetable, but her stomach quickly rejects it.

Slowly, Scarlett rises and, with her fist clenched toward heaven, she vows: "As God is my witness, they're not going to lick me . . . I'm going to live through this and when it's over I'm never going to be hungry again. No, nor any of my folks! If I have to lie, steal, cheat or kill, as God is my witness I'll never be hungry again."

Cut and print it. Sounds easy enough, but it wasn't, not by a long shot.

Selznick envisioned the scene ending with Scarlett in silhouette against a clear dawn sky. To achieve this, the crew planned to film at the Lasky Mesa in the San Fernando Valley. There the crew laid down a track on which the camera could pull back to capture the long shot of Scarlett, that is, if Mother Nature cooperated.

The shot had to be filmed on a mistless morning in an area of the Valley famous for mists rolling in from the Pacific. So a member of the crew stationed himself on the Mesa in the wee hours of the new day to watch the sky. By 2:30 A.M., if the conditions looked hopeful, the sentinel headed for the nearest phone to sound the alert. Vivien Leigh, the director, and camera crew were then awakened and rushed to the wet, chilly Mesa. With their eyes on the horizon, everyone held their breath as they waited for the shot to appear, usually around 4 A.M.

On the days the mist rolled in, all efforts were for nought. When the crew did manage to capture the shot on a clear morning, Selznick thought they could do better and ordered another stakeout at the Mesa. Leigh and the crew made nearly a dozen trips to the hilltop in the two months it took to capture this shot. Even then Selznick was still not satisfied, so he ended up splicing together footage from several not-quite-perfect takes.

Leigh didn't mind getting up that early in the morning for the shot. What she did object to was her response to the radish: retching. She argued with Selznick about eliminating this "unladylike" action from the scene; he wanted to keep it in. Finally they compromised. The action would stay in, but Leigh could dub in the sound at the studio.

At the studio, Leigh's rendition of retching for the sound editor was unconvincing. Olivia de Havilland thought she could do a better job and proceeded to demonstrate. Hal Kern, the editor, was so impressed he substituted de Havilland's sound effects for Leigh's in the soundtrack.

THE DAY CLARK GABLE CRIED

According to the script, Scarlett has fallen down the staircase and has suffered a miscarriage. A distraught, unshaven Rhett, alone in his room, blames himself for what has happened. But Melanie soon brings news that Scarlett is better. Rhett, filled with relief and remorse, covers his face with his hands and weeps.

"I can't do it!" Clark Gable complained to Olivia de Havilland during rehearsals for the scene. "I won't do it! I'm going to leave acting . . . I'll quit pictures, starting with this one!"

MELANIE AND RHETT.

De Havilland tried her best to encourage him, but Gable was resolute. Leading men in the 1930s just did not cry on screen, and Gable would rather abandon his career than risk the humiliation of audiences laughing at him.

Gable appealed to Fleming. Have the scene rewritten, he begged. Or better still, eliminate the scene entirely from the picture. Fleming privately assured Gable that crying would create more audience sympathy for Rhett, but Gable was not convinced.

On the day of filming, an edgy and agitated Gable arrived on the set. He again threatened to walk off the picture, but Fleming proposed a compromise. The scene would be shot two ways: one with tears and the other simply showing a bereft Rhett's back. Whichever Gable thought to be the stronger scene would be used. Gable was only partly relieved.

Fleming cleared the set of visitors and extraneous crew members, and filmed the two versions in only two takes: the eloquent back first and then the tears. After Gable saw the rushes, he was amazed at his performance. He agreed that the weeping scene was more effective and okayed its use in the film.

GWTW'S FILMING: AN ENDURANCE TEST FOR ITS STARS

The official shooting of *GWTW* began on January 26, 1939 and ended five months and one day later on June 27, 1939. The stars endured grueling six-day workweeks filled with sixteen-hour days. Here's how long *GWTW*'s stars were at it: Vivien Leigh, 125 days; Clark Gable, 71 days; Olivia de Havilland, 59 days; and Leslie Howard, 32 days.

Filming Ends, Sort Of

Selznick was under pressure from Louis B. Mayer to give *GWTW* a happy ending. Mayer was in favor of a concluding scene showing Scarlett rushing after Rhett, calling his name, and a fade-out shot of them in a loving embrace. Selznick, though, wanted to leave audiences with only the same glimmer of hope that Margaret Mitchell had left with her readers: that Scarlett would, somehow, get him back.

Selznick rewrote the final scene several times. Finally, on the night before the scene was shot, he achieved the version he wanted. As it appears on the screen, Scarlett watches Rhett walk down the front path, put on his hat, and disappear into the mist.

"I can't let him go. I can't. There must be some way to bring him back," she cries. "Oh, I can't think about this now. I'll go crazy if I do. I'll think about it tomorrow." She closes the heavy front door and walks toward the staircase. "But I must think about it, I must think about it. What is there to do? What is there that matters?"

With heart-wrenching sobs, she sinks to the staircase in a flood of tears. Then she hears the voices of her father, Ashley, and Rhett reminding her that she still has Tara.

She slowly rises from the staircase as well as from her despair, and as the camera pulls in for the close-up she says: "Tara ... home. I'll go home, and I'll think of some way to get him back. After all, tomorrow is another day." Then, as the film ends, a pull-back shot catches a silhouetted Scarlett with bonnet in hand, looking at Tara.

With that last scene, the official filming schedule ended on June 27, 1939. Selznick sent a telegram to Jock Whitney stating, "Sound the siren. Scarlett O'Hara completed her performance at noon today." That evening, the cast and crew attended the traditional "wrap party," but there was additional work to be done. Selznick ordered the reshooting of certain scenes. The special effects unit was still hard at work, and other fill-in sequences had to be filmed. The filming of *GWTW* had ended, sort of.

Postproduction of *GWTW*

While scenes were being reshot and special effects orchestrated, Selznick busied himself with screening the existing footage and selecting takes of scenes. The selected scenes were assembled, and by mid-July, with the assistance of film editor Hal Kern, Selznick had a rough cut of the film. But the running time was six hours. Then came the process of eliminating this scene and cutting that entrance to shorten the film to a manageable length.

The work was intense. Selznick and Kern spent interminable hours in the cutting room (one session lasted almost forty-eight hours!) until Selznick had a five-hour version that he showed to cast and crew. It was at this showing that Selznick presented to each of his stars a leather-bound copy of the script. But this script was not the multicolored mess that had been used for shooting. Selznick had Lydia Schiller, the continuity girl, compile the "official" script from the edited version of the film.

Selznick went back to the cutting room and eliminated another hour from the film. In late August he showed this second rough-cut version to Louis B. Mayer and other MGM executives. Although Mayer had to excuse himself several times for visits to the men's room, he was enthusiastic about the film.

The film needed narrative titles to bridge one part of the film with another, so Selznick turned to Ben Hecht for this job. Hecht succeeded in writing in the flowery style (e.g., "There was a land of cavaliers and cotton fields called the Old South") that Selznick favored.

For the film's title, Selznick wanted "the biggest main title that has ever been made." To achieve this, each word of the title was hand painted on a sheet of plate glass. The camera was mounted on a dolly, and it pulled the camera along as it photographed the four plate-glass sheets.

Selznick continued to add new footage and to trim existing footage of the film. So from day to day the running time of *GWTW* went up and down like the proverbial yo-yo. Finally, Selznick managed to reduce the film to 20,300 feet, which gave a running time of three hours and forty minutes—the length of the final version.

SNEAK PEEKS

By September, Selznick was ready to preview *GWTW*. Because the film was not completely finished, he didn't want to attract the attention of the press, so plans for the preview were super hush-hush.

The first preview took place in Riverside, California. Selznick, an entourage, and twenty-four cans of film arrived at the Riverside Theater on Saturday, September 9. The audience was told that instead of the expected feature, they were about to see a very long movie. People were given the chance to leave if they wished, but they were warned that once the film started no one would be allowed to exit or to enter the theater.

Murmurs of anticipation rose among the audience. As the title swept across the screen, moviegoers were on their feet with shouts of joy. They jumped to their feet again four hours later when the film ended and gave Selznick a thunderous ovation. Selznick, his wife, and Jock Whitney wiped tears from their eyes. Later Selznick called the evening a "sensational success. The reaction was everything that we hoped for and expected."

In mid-October, a second preview was held. The Santa Barbara audience was just as wild with excitement as the Riverside audience had been.

Selznick was thrilled when he read the review cards filled out by the audiences. "The greatest picture ever made," said one. "The greatest picture since *Birth of a Nation*," said another. "The screen's greatest achievement of all times," a third noted. But audiences also made critical comments, especially about missing Rhett Butler's "damn" exit line. Selznick paid attention to the audience's negative comments and took the film back into the cutting room for more editing.

MUSIC BY
MAX STEINER

In October 1939, Selznick selected Warner Brothers composer Max Steiner to compose the score for *GWTW*. Vienna-born Steiner, who was the godson of composer Richard Strauss, was well known for his work on *Jezebel*, *A Star is Born*, *Garden of Allah*, and *King Kong*. Selznick told Steiner he wanted "instead of two or three hours of original music, little original music and a score based on the great music of the world, and of the South in particular."

Steiner ignored Selznick's request. The score he composed contained mostly original music, but he did use some Southern favorites such as "Dixie" and "The Bonnie Blue Flag" as well as military and patriotic tunes. Steiner wrote separate themes for Tara and for the leading characters. He also included love themes for the relationships between Melanie and Ashley, Scarlett and Ashley, and Scarlett and Rhett.

Since Selznick feared that Steiner would not be able to meet the short deadline he had been given, Selznick hired composer and conductor Franz Waxman to write an "insurance score." Selznick wasn't pleased with Waxman's work. The producer discreetly talked to Herbert Stothard, MGM's musical director and composer, about taking over the score. Unfortunately, Stothard blabbed that he was taking over for Steiner. This got back to Steiner, and all hell broke loose.

But as a result, Steiner increased his output, and this in turn pleased Selznick who advised the composer to "just go mad with schmaltz in the last three reels." Steiner ignored this piece of advice, too, and as a result the lushly orchestrated, richly textured score that Steiner produced for *GWTW* was a movie masterpiece.

Musical Notes

• "Mammy's Theme" is the first heard in the film. It occurs when the credit appears for MGM and Technicolor.

• The most famous theme that Steiner composed was "Tara's Theme." The music was later adapted for the popular song, "My Own True Love."

• Steiner did not write a separate theme for Ashley. Instead, the "elegant Mr. Wilkes" was surrounded musically by the two women who loved him in the "Melanie and Ashley Theme" and the "Scarlett and Ashley Theme."

• Steiner borrowed the melody for "Melanie's Theme" from his score of the 1934 RKO film *The Fountain*.

• Steiner used touches of Stephen Foster tunes in *GWTW*'s score. In one humorous instance, Steiner used the Foster melody "Massa's in de Cold, Cold Ground" for the scene in which Scarlett, as the newly widowed Mrs. Hamilton, tries on a stylish purple bonnet.

• Selznick insisted that segments of MGM stock music remain in the film after the previews. These were used in the scenes "Approach of the Yankee Deserter," "Shantytown," and "Rhett Carries Scarlett Upstairs."

• Steiner, under intense pressure from Selznick to complete the score, turned to his colleagues for some help. Franz Waxman, Adolph Deutsch, and Hugo Friedhofer contributed, and Heinz Roemheld composed the music that accompanied the escape from Atlanta and the burning of the depot.

• Selznick suggested to record companies the idea of recording an album of *GWTW*'s music from Steiner's soundtracks. Unbelievably, the record companies turned down the idea. Although symphonic re-recordings were produced later, they lacked the beauty of the Steiner originals.

THAT DAMN WORD "DAMN"

In the novel, Rhett leaves a tearful Scarlett who wails, "If you go, where shall I go, what shall I do?" And Gable steals the scene with the immortal words: "My dear, I don't give a damn." At the outset, Selznick knew he would have problems with that damn word "damn."

The Motion Picture Production Code developed in 1930 by the Association of Motion Picture Producers barred from the screen, among other things, the use of profanity. Specifically, it forbade the use of the word "damn."

Sidney Howard, aware of the industry's censorship code, changed the line to "My dear, I don't care." But Selznick knew how much the American public would expect the line to be left intact, so he ordered the scene shot with each version of the line. At the last moment, Selznick added the word "frankly" to the beginning of Rhett's line because he felt the word added an offhanded quality to the delivery.

The censor, Joseph Breen, refused to permit Gable's stronger version, so preview audiences heard the "I-don't-care" line. They expressed their disappointment on the preview cards they handed back to Selznick, so he decided to appeal to a higher power.

Selznick wrote to Will H. Hays, the head of the Motion Pictures Producers, and stated that the *Oxford English Dictionary* described "damn" not as an oath or curse but as a vulgarism. Selznick also pointed to the public's general acceptance of the word by citing magazines such as *Woman's Home Companion*, *Saturday Evening Post*, and *Collier's*, which used the word frequently. Last, he noted the disappointment of preview audiences. "On our very fade-out it gives an impression of unfaithfulness after three hours and forty-five minutes of extreme fidelity to Miss Mitchell's work." (The final cut was five minutes shorter.)

Hays must have recognized a good argument when he saw one. He reversed Breen's decision and allowed Selznick to use the line that has become as famous as Scarlett's "I'll think about that tomorrow." But since Selznick was technically in violation of the Production Code, he was fined $5,000. He felt it was worth every penny.

FACTS AND FIGURES

Production
- 250,000 man-hours spent in preproduction
- 750,000 man-hours spent during production

Footage
- 449,512 feet of film shot
- 160,000 feet of film printed
- 20,300 feet of film in the final version
- 220 minutes of running time

Actors
- 59 leading and supporting cast members
- 2,400 extras

Animals
- 1,100 horses
- 375 pigs, mules, oxen, cows, dogs, and other animals

Vehicles
- 450 vehicles, including wagons, ambulances, and gun caissons

Sets
- 3,000 sketches drawn of major scenes
- 200 sets designed
- 90 sets built using 1,000,000 feet of lumber

Costs
- $3,700,000 actual production cost
- $4,250,000 total cost including overheads for prints, publicity, advertising, etc.

TEST YOUR
GWTW KNOWLEDGE

◆

THE GREATEST MOVIE
OF ALL TIME

1. With whom is Scarlett chatting on the front porch of Tara, as the film opens?

2. What secret did they share with Scarlett?

3. During evening prayers, what did Scarlett decide to do?

4. What did Mammy and Scarlett argue about on the morning of the barbecue?

5. At the barbecue, who told Scarlett about Rhett Butler's reputation?

6. From what school has Rhett been expelled?

7. What does a spurned Scarlett break in the Twelve Oaks library? Whom does this rouse from the sofa?

8. Who had been Scarlett's first husband?

9. What caused his death?

10. At the Atlanta Bazaar, how much did Rhett bid for the honor of leading the opening reel with Scarlett?

11. Who fainted after Scarlett accepted Rhett's bid to dance?

12. What present did Rhett bring to Scarlett from Paris?

13. How long was Ashley's Christmas leave?

14. What was Ashley's rank?

15. What promise did Ashley extract from Scarlett before he returned to the war?

16. What did Belle Watling give to Melanie outside the Atlanta hospital?

17. Where was Belle's establishment located?

18. For whom did Scarlett search among the wounded soldiers? Why did she need him?

19. Who lied about having childbirthing skills?

20. What did Melanie want to bring on the escape to Tara?

21. Why did Rhett abandon Scarlett on the road to Tara?

22. By the time Scarlett arrived at Tara, who had died from typhoid?

23. What did Scarlett vow in Tara's vegetable garden?

24. Whom does Scarlett shoot on Tara's staircase?

25. How much money did Scarlett need for the taxes on Tara?

26. Who threatened to buy Tara when the plantation was sold at the sheriff's sale?

27. Whom had he married?

28. Where did Scarlett obtain the material for her Atlanta gown?

29. From whom did Scarlett plan to get the needed tax money?

30. What gave away Scarlett's destitution in the Atlanta jail?

31. To save Tara, whom did Scarlett marry? Whom was he supposed to marry?

32. Where did this sign appear: "The war is over. Don't ask for credit"?

33. In what other business enterprise did Scarlett engage?

34. Where was Scarlett attacked? Who rescued her?

35. Who were the members of the evening sewing circle?

36. What book did Melanie read to the sewing circle?

37. Who was wounded during the raid to avenge Scarlett's attack?

38. What did Rhett do when he called on Scarlett after Frank Kennedy's funeral?

39. What gift did Rhett bring back from New Orleans for Mammy?

40. What was Scarlett's waist measurement after giving birth to Bonnie?

41. Who found Scarlett in Ashley's arms?

42. What social function did Rhett force Scarlett to attend alone that evening?

43. The following day, where did Rhett announce he was taking Bonnie?

44. Why was their trip cut short?
45. What caused Scarlett's miscarriage?
46. Why did Rhett warn Bonnie not to jump?
47. Who convinced Rhett to schedule Bonnie's funeral?
48. What was Ashley holding when Scarlett left the dying Melanie's room?
49. Where did Rhett say he was going when he left Scarlett?
50. What did Scarlett decide to do after Rhett walked out?

THE CURIOUS NUMBER OF SCENES THAT TAKE PLACE ON STAIRCASES

On the staircase at Tara

• From the window on the landing, Mammy spots Ellen O'Hara returning home and grumbles about her ministering to the white trash Slattery family.

• Scarlett learns from Mammy about Tara's devastation at the hands of the Yankee invaders.

• Scarlett orders the ailing Melanie back to bed when she offers to help with the plantation work.

• Scarlett confronts and shoots the Yankee deserter.

On the staircase at Twelve Oaks

• Ashley greets Scarlett as she arrives for the barbecue.

• Scarlett flirts with Frank Kennedy and flatters him about his "new set of whiskers."

• Scarlett encounters the Tarleton twins and convinces them to "eat barbecue" with her.

• Scarlett sees Rhett Butler for the first time.

• Scarlett eavesdrops on the men talking over brandy and cigars about the war.

• Scarlett overhears Melanie defending Scarlett's flirting with all the men at the barbecue.

• Charles Hamilton proposes marriage to Scarlett.

THE KOBAL COLLECTION/MGM

 CHARLES HAMILTON GREETS SCARLETT
ON THE STAIRS AT TWELVE OAKS.

• Scarlett views the destruction of Twelve Oaks on her way home to Tara with Melanie, the baby, and Prissy.

On the staircase at Aunt Pittypat's house

• Melanie explains how she obtained the material for Ashley's Christmas tunic and asks him to make sure it doesn't get torn.

• Scarlett asks to accompany Ashley to the train station at the end of his Christmas leave.

• When she discovers Melanie in labor, Scarlett sends Prissy to fetch Dr. Meade.

• Scarlett threatens to sell Prissy South for not finding Dr. Meade.

• Scarlett slaps Prissy when she reveals her lack of childbirthing skills.

• Scarlett holds a lantern for Rhett as he carries Melanie out to the carriage to escape Atlanta.

• Rhett greets Scarlett after Frank Kennedy's funeral and notices she has been drinking.

On staircases here and there

• Lists of Gettysburg casualties are handed to the crowd from the staircase at the newspaper office.

• Belle Watling approaches Melanie and Scarlett with a contribution on the staircase outside the Atlanta church-turned-hospital.

• Melanie chats with a ragged Confederate soldier on the back steps of Tara and learns that Ashley was taken prisoner.

On the staircase at Scarlett's Atlanta house

• Scarlett hears a drunken Rhett invite her to come into the dining room.

• Rhett sweeps Scarlett into his arms for a night of passion.

• Scarlett admits to Rhett that she is pregnant and, in attempting to strike him, misses and tumbles down the stairs.

• Mammy asks Melanie to speak to Rhett about funeral services for Bonnie.

• Rhett bids farewell to Scarlett as he leaves for Charleston.

• A tearful Scarlett decides that "tomorrow is another day."

THE PLAYERS WHO'S WHO

Match the character in column 1 with the actor or actress who immortalized the role in column 2.

Column 1	Column 2
1. Mammy	a. Vivien Leigh
2. Aunt Pittypat Hamilton	b. Alicia Rhett
3. Rhett Butler	c. Eddie Anderson
4. Jonas Wilkerson	d. Rand Brooks
5. Prissy	e. Laura Hope Crews
6. Scarlett O'Hara	f. Olivia de Havilland
7. Stuart Tarleton	g. Harry Davenport
8. Ellen O'Hara	h. Hattie McDaniel
9. Ashley Wilkes	i. Victor Jory
10. Uncle Peter	j. Carroll Nye
11. Belle Watling	k. Ann Rutherford
12. Melanie Hamilton	l. Everett Brown
13. Gerald O'Hara	m. George Reeves
14. Big Sam	n. Butterfly McQueen
15. India Wilkes	o. Ona Munson
16. Frank Kennedy	p. Clark Gable
17. Dr. Meade	q. Barbara O'Neil
18. Mrs. Merriwether	r. Leslie Howard
19. Bonnie Butler	s. Thomas Mitchell
20. Carreen O'Hara	t. Jane Darwell
21. Charles Hamilton	u. Ward Bond
22. Tom, the Yankee captain	v. Cammie King

WHO SAID IT? (#1)

From the following list of characters, decide who spoke the line of movie dialogue.

Scarlett O'Hara Rhett Butler
Melanie Hamilton Wilkes Ashley Wilkes

1. "Has the war started?"
2. "Fine thing when a horse can get shoes and humans can't."

3. "She's the only dream I ever had that didn't die in the face of reality."

4. "Here, take my handkerchief. Never at any crisis of your life have I known you to have a handkerchief."

5. "Do you think it would be dishonest if we went through his haversack?"

6. "Panic's a pretty sight, isn't it."

7. "You must be brave. You must. How else can I bear going?"

8. "I've always thought a good lashing with a buggy whip would benefit you immensely."

9. "You will take good care of it, won't you. You won't let it get torn. Promise me."

10. "It's cold, and I left my muff at home. Would you mind if I put my hand in your pocket?"

11. "Oh, can't we go away and forget we ever said these things?"

12. "You go into the arena alone. The lions are hungry for you."

13. "Isn't it enough that you've gathered every other man's heart today? You've always had mine. You cut your teeth on it."

14. "You've lived in dirt so long you can't understand anything else, and you're jealous of something you can't understand."

15. "This war stopped being a joke when a girl like you doesn't know how to wear the latest fashion."

16. "Don't cry. She mustn't see you've been crying."

17. "Nobody cares about me. You all act as though it were nothing at all."

18. "Most of the miseries of the world were caused by wars. And when the wars were over no one ever knew what they were about."

19. "Boys aren't any use to anybody. Don't you think I'm proof of that?"

20. "Take a good look, my dear. It's an historic moment. You can tell your grandchildren how you watched the Old South disappear one night."

21. "I'm too young to be a widow."

22. "You have so much life. I've always admired you so. I wish I could be more like you."

23. "With enough courage you can do without a reputation."

24. "You seem to belong here. As if it had all been imagined for you."

25. "Frankly, my dear, I don't give a damn."

26. "Don't worry about me. I can shoot straight, if I don't have to shoot too far."

27. "It's a pity we couldn't have fought the war out in a poker game. You'd have done better than General Grant with far less effort."

28. "Don't look back. It drags at your heart until you can't do anything but look back."

29. "The happiest days are when babies come."

30. "How could I help loving you. You who have all the passion for life that I lack."

31. "I'll go home, and I'll think of some way to get him back."

32. "I shall be proud to speak to you. Proud to be under obligation to you."

33. "Selfish to the end, aren't you? Thinking only of your own precious hide with never a thought for the noble Cause."

34. "War, war, war. This war talk's spoiling all the fun at every party this spring. I get so bored I could scream."

THE KOBAL COLLECTION/MGM

 GABLE DISCUSSING THE WAR WITH THE MEN AT TWELVE OAKS ON THE AFTERNOON OF THE BARBECUE.

35. "Any of you beauties know where I can steal a horse for a good cause?"

36. "I'll hate you till I die. I can't think of anything bad enough to call you."

37. "Tonight I wouldn't mind dancing with Abe Lincoln himself."

38. "I seem to be spoiling everybody's brandy and cigars and dreams of victory."

39. "I could never hate you. And I know you must care about me. Oh you do care, don't you?"

40. "I'll think about that tomorrow."

41. "All we've got is cotton, and slaves, and arrogance."

42. "My life is over. Nothing will ever happen to me anymore."

THE MASTER'S *GWTW* GAME: MINOR CHARACTERS MATCH

This game is designed to separate the true Windie from the mere fanatic. Match the actor or actress in column A with the minor role undertaken in *GWTW* in column B.

Column A	Column B
1. Mary Anderson	a. Bonnie's London nurse
2. Irving Bacon	b. Shantytown attacker
3. Yakima Canutt	c. Mrs. Meade
4. Cliff Edwards	d. Phil Meade
5. Robert Elliott	e. Maybelle Merriwether
6. Olin Howland	f. Reminiscent soldier in Atlanta hospital
7. Paul Hurst	g. The Yankee deserter
8. Lillian Kemble-Cooper	h. The Yankee major
9. J.M. Kerrigan	i. The Yankee corporal
10. Mickey Kuhn	j. Johnnie Gallegher
11. Jackie Moran	k. A Yankee businessman
12. Leona Roberts	l. Beau Wilkes

WHO SAID IT? (#2)

From the following list of characters, decide who spoke the line of movie dialogue.

Gerald O'Hara	India Wilkes
Ellen O'Hara	Cathleen Calvert
Suellen O'Hara	Charles Hamilton
Carreen O'Hara	Frank Kennedy

1. "Why land is the only thing in the world worth working for, worth fighting for, worth dying for because it's the only thing that lasts."

2. "How is Ashley today, Scarlett? He didn't seem to be paying much attention to you."

3. "Are you hinting, Mr. Butler, that the Yankees can lick us?"

4. "What difference does it make who you marry so long as he's a Southerner and thinks like you?"

5. "She's had three husbands, and I'll be an old maid."

6. "It's only natural to want to look young and be young when you are young."

7. "I've been waiting here two whole days. And I've got to tell her that I was wrong about something."

8. "My dear, don't you know? That's Rhett Butler. He's from Charleston. He has the most terrible reputation."

9. "She can get mad quicker than any woman I ever saw."

10. "I do hate you. You've done all you could to lower the prestige of decent people."

11. "Bonds. They're all we've saved. All we have left. Bonds."

12. "What happened this afternoon was just what you deserved. And if there was any justice, you'd have gotten worse."

13. "I guess things like hands and ladies don't matter so much any more."

14. "If true love carries any weight with you, you can be sure your sister will be rich in that."

15. "Don't cry, darling. The war'll be over in a few weeks, and I'll be coming back to you."

16. "You act on me just like a tonic."

17. "You mustn't think unkindly of her. She's made it possible for us to keep Tara always."

I'LL THINK ABOUT THAT TOMORROW

GWTW is peppered with Scarlett's favorite expressions such as "Fiddle-dee-dee" and "Great balls of fire." But she uttered her most famous screen oath only three times.

1. At the opening when the Tarletons ask if she is planning to eat barbecue with them the next day: "Well I haven't thought about that yet. I'll think about that tomorrow."

2. After shooting the Yankee deserter: "Well I guess I've done murder. Oh, I won't think about that now. I'll think about that tomorrow."

3. After Rhett walks out: "I can't let him go. I can't. There must be some way to bring him back. Oh, I can't think about that now. I'll go crazy if I do. I'll think about it tomorrow."

And, of course, the final lines of the movie contain an unforgettable variation of Scarlett's purposeful procrastination theme. After she hears the disembodied voices of her father, Ashley, and Rhett on the staircase, she says: "Tara . . . Home. I'll go home, and I'll think of some way to get him back. After all, tomorrow is another day."

WHO SAID IT? (#3)

From the following list of characters, decide who spoke the line of movie dialogue.

Aunt Pittypat Hamilton Mrs. Merriwether
Uncle Peter Bonnie Butler
Dr. Meade Beau Wilkes
Mrs. Meade

1. "Go on, you trash. Don't you be pestering these ladies."

2. "Why do I have to go back to bed? It's morning."

3. "Good heavens, woman, this is war not a garden party."

4. "I will so jump. I can jump better than ever because I've grown. And I've moved the bar higher."

5. "Don't go getting so uppity. Even if you is the last chicken in Atlanta."

6. "For a widow to appear in public at a social gathering—everytime I think of it I feel faint."

7. "London Bridge! Will it be falling down?"

8. "Were you really there? What did it look like? Does she have cut-glass chandeliers, plush curtains, and dozens of mirrors?"

9. "Where is my mother going away to, and why can't I go along, please."

10. "There must be a great deal of good in a man who would love a child so much."

11. "I may be a coward but, oh dear, Yankees in Georgia! How did they ever get in!"

GWTW GOOFS

Here and there in *GWTW* are minor mistakes that resulted either from errors in continuity or from slips in the editing process. Did you catch or miss any of these *GWTW* goofs?

1. "I wore this old dress just because I thought you liked it."

   Scarlett delivers this line to the Tarleton boys on the staircase at Twelve Oaks on the morning of the barbecue. Audiences might have wondered when the boys had previously seen her in her green-sprigged, flowered muslin dress.

   When the original opening scene of the movie was shot in January 1939, Scarlett was flirting with the Tarletons in this very same gown. However, by June, Selznick decided to reshoot this scene and have Scarlett wear the white gown she wore during Evening Prayers. So since the dress she wore to the barbecue was not the one they had seen her in the afternoon before, her line to the Tarletons lost all its meaning.

2. Scarlett's coral necklace.

   When Mammy helps Scarlett dress for the barbecue, there is clearly no coral necklace gracing Scarlett's throat. And in the rush to hurry through her hotcakes and to fetch her thrown-aside parasol before her father counts to ten, there is no time for Scarlett to snatch up a piece of jewelry. Yet Scarlett is wearing the necklace when Mammy

THE KOBAL COLLECTION/MGM

SCARLETT WEARING HER ON-AGAIN,
OFF-AGAIN CORAL NECKLACE.

helps her undress for her nap at Twelve Oaks. The necklace can even be seen ever so slightly a bit earlier when Scarlett climbs the Twelve Oaks staircase with Cathleen Calvert. The strange appearance of Scarlett's coral necklace is clearly a continuity error.

3. Shadows out of sync.

The shadow scene in which Scarlett and Melanie care for the wounded in the Atlanta hospital was filmed with two doubles. Since Leigh and de Havilland were standing at the wrong angle to cast the shadows, two stand-ins were positioned in front of a high-intensity light. The shadows of the doubles were reflected on the wall in back of the stars, and the result was a stunning visual effect. Yet upon closer look, the gestures of the stand-ins are not totally synchronized with the movements of the stars. Shadows out of sync is a goof picked up by only the most avid viewer.

4. Scarlett's black mourning bonnet.

Scarlett's flight from Atlanta is so sudden that, as she leaves Aunt Pittypat's house, she is hatless. Curiously, though, a black mourning bonnet appears on her head as she and Rhett ride through the depot area. The hat remains in place through the encounter with the looters, during the fire, and as she and Rhett follow the retreating Confederate troops outside the city. In the next scene, when Rhett stops the carriage on the turn to Tara, the bonnet vanishes. The sudden appearance and equally sudden disappearance of Scarlett's black mourning bonnet is another error in continuity.

5. Gerald's reprimand.

In Tara's Cotton Patch scene, Scarlett speaks sharply to and slaps her sister, Suellen. Immediately afterward, Gerald reprimands Scarlett for her ill treatment of the servants. Is this a non sequitur? No, it's another glitch in continuity. Scenes showing an acid-tongued Scarlett speaking to Mammy, Pork, and Prissy were edited out, yet Gerald's admonition remained.

6. Scarlett's breakfast tray.

After her night of passion with Rhett, Scarlett awakens and delights in the memory of the ravishment. Mammy enters, comes to the bedside and takes away a tray containing a silver service. An earlier part of this scene showed Bonnie bringing the breakfast tray to her mother, but this was deleted during the editing. Without this segment, audiences were left to wonder whether part of Rhett's romantic overtures included a midnight supper.

WHO SAID IT? (#4)

From the following list of characters, decide who spoke the line of movie dialogue.

Pork	Yankee deserter at Tara
Prissy	Tom, a Yankee captain
Mammy	Belle Watling
Big Sam	Shantytown attacker
Jonas Wilkerson	A Yankee major
Johnnie Gallegher	

1. "We finished plowing the creek bottom today. What do you want me to start on tomorrow?"

2. "I told him you was prostrate with grief."

3. "She's a mighty cold woman. Prancing about Atlanta by herself. She killed her husband same as if she shot him."

4. "He's her husband, ain't he?"

5. "You might as well take my money, Miz Wilkes. It's good money even if it is mine."

6. "Does you know a dyed-hair woman?"

7. "It's hard to be strict with a man who loses money so pleasantly."

8. "What gentlemens says and what they thinks is two different things. And I ain't noticed Mist' Ashley asking for to marry you."

9. "I don't know nothin' 'bout birthin' babies."

10. "Regular little spitfire, ain't you."

11. "Savannah would be better for you. You'll just get in trouble in Atlanta."

12. "The whole Confederate army's got the same troubles—crawlin' clothes and dysentery."

13. "There ain't never been a lady in this town nice to me like you was."

14. "Ma says that if you puts a knife under the bed it cuts the pain in two."

15. "There ain't no barn no more, Miz Scarlett. The Yankees done burned it for firewood."

16. "We came out here to pay a call, a friendly call, and talk a little business with old friends."

17. "There's your new mill hands, Mrs. Kennedy. The pick of all the best jails in Georgia."

18. "Can you give me a quarter?"

19. "Horse, make tracks."

20. "It's about time you Rebels learned you can't take the law into your own hands."

A UNIQUE MOVIE

What is unique about *GWTW*? It's a Civil War movie that never shows any battle scenes. The audience sees only the effects of war:

- The anxious crowds waiting for the Gettysburg casualty lists
- Trains of incoming wounded as Ashley arrives for Christmas leave
- Ashley's discouraged end-of-the-war speech to Scarlett
- Scarlett and Melanie caring for the wounded and dying in the Atlanta hospital
- The shelling of Atlanta and panic in the streets
- The multitude of wounded at the depot
- The burning of the Atlanta depot
- The Confederate army in retreat from Atlanta
- Scarlett hiding under the bridge with soldiers passing above
- Scarlett and Prissy on their way to Tara crossing a battlefield filled with dead soldiers
- Scarlett viewing the ruins of Twelve Oaks and returning to the ravaged Tara
- The montage of soldiers and cannons that opens Part Two
- The trespassing Yankee deserter at Tara
- The delousing of Frank Kennedy and feeding the returning "starving scarecrows"
- News that Ashley has been taken prisoner
- Gerald's announcing that the war is over

THE *WIND* SWEEPS AMERICA

◆

PLANS FOR THE PREMIERE

As Selznick worked round the clock to complete *GWTW*, MGM, who would release the film, made plans for the film's premiere. Selznick

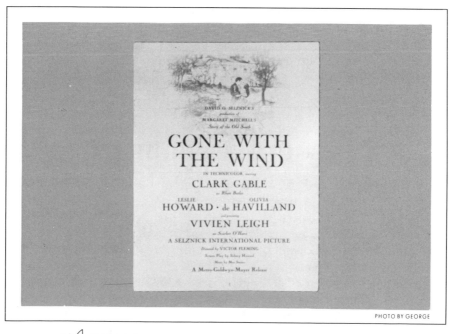

PHOTO BY GEORGE

THE PROGRAM FOR THE ATLANTA PREMIERE.

wanted to make sure it went perfectly, so he bombarded MGM's publicity director Howard Dietz with endless memos and telegrams concerning every phase of the premiere. In one cable, Selznick noted: "I want you to be very careful of the paper you select for the program—stop—Sometimes their crackling noise makes it difficult to hear the dialogue—stop—promise you will attend to this."

The world's premiere was scheduled for Friday, December 15, 1939 in Margaret Mitchell's hometown, Atlanta. In honor of the film's debut, the governor of Georgia, Eurith D. Rivers, proclaimed the day of the premiere an official state holiday. Not wanting to be a slouch, the mayor of Atlanta, William B. Hartsfield, proclaimed a municipal half-day holiday and ordered three days of celebrations including parades, citizens dressing up in period costumes, and a Junior League Ball.

The site of the premiere would be the Loew's Grand Theatre on Peachtree Street. The facade of the 2,500-seat theater was false-fronted with giant white columns to make it resemble Twelve Oaks. High above street level was a two-story-high portrait of Vivien Leigh and Clark Gable.

Tickets for the gala event, which were selling for $10 apiece, quickly sold out, and scalpers got as much as $200 for a single ticket as the day of the premiere drew closer. Nearly one million visitors filled the city and battled for rooms in Atlanta's hotels and guest cottages. Citizens of Atlanta agreed that the hometown premiere of *GWTW* was the biggest thing to hit the city since William Tecumseh Sherman.

On December 11, just four days before the Atlanta premiere, Selznick sent this wire to Kay Brown, who had preceded her boss to the premiere city: "Have just finished Gone With the Wind. God bless us one and all."

THE ATLANTA FESTIVITIES

On Thursday, December 14, the governor of Georgia and the mayor of Atlanta headed the airport contingent that welcomed the Selznick entourage. Selznick was accompanied by his wife Irene, his brother Myron, Vivien Leigh, Laurence Olivier, Olivia de Havilland, Evelyn Keyes, and Ona Munson. Conspicuously absent were Leslie Howard, Clark Gable, and Victor Fleming.

Howard had returned to England in August after war was declared in Europe. Fleming had decided to boycott the premiere after reading a newspaper publicity story. In the story, Selznick was quoted as saying he had supervised all the directors of the film. This was the last straw for an enraged Fleming, who broke off all further relations with Selznick.

Gable had decided to support Fleming and boycott the film as well until he was convinced by MGM to attend. But Gable couldn't stand the thought of spending the long flight in Selznick's company so he, his wife Carole Lombard, and a group of MGM executives flew to Atlanta separately in a DC-3. On the side of Gable's plane were the words "Gone With the Wind" painted in large letters.

A forty-piece band struck up "Dixie" as the two Hollywood contingents landed at the bunting- and Confederate-flag-draped airport. As Vivien Leigh walked down the red carpet amid the crush of reporters and popping flashbulbs, she recognized the tune being played by the band. "Oh, they're playing the song from the picture," she said. A quick-thinking Howard Dietz, who didn't want the comment attributed to Scarlett O'Hara, told a reporter who had overheard the remark that Olivia de Havilland had said it.

The luminaries were ushered into open-topped cars for the motorcade trip to the Georgian Terrace Hotel. Along the Peachtree Street route, throngs of people (some dressed in contemporary clothing but many

UPI/BETTMAN ARCHIVE

 MARGARET MITCHELL SURROUNDED BY LEIGH, GABLE, SELZNICK, AND DE HAVILLAND IN ATLANTA.

in hoop skirts and Confederate uniforms) cheered, shouted the rebel yell, and waved flags at the celebrities.

When the motorcade arrived at the hotel, the mayor officially welcomed the stars and introduced them to the crowd, which broke into renewed pandemonium. Confetti flew, and giant spotlights lit up the mayor as he presented his guests with Wedgwood coffee-and-tea sets.

Later that evening, the Hollywood stars were the guests of honor at a Junior League charity ball held at the Atlanta Municipal Auditorium. The set of the Atlanta Bazaar had been flown in from Selznick's studio and erected for the ball, and the stars arrived in costume. The Kay Kyser Orchestra began a lilting waltz, and Gable, dressed in his blockade-runner's suit, shared the dance with Mayor Hartsfield's daughter.

All of the stars were anxious to meet the author of *GWTW*. However, Margaret Mitchell had decided to settle an old score with the Junior League that had denied her membership so many years before. She had sent regrets that she would not be able to attend the ball.

The next day, December 15, was kicked off with a luncheon given by Governor Rivers for the governors of Tennessee, Alabama, Florida, and South Carolina, who were to attend the premiere. The luncheon was followed by a tea at the governor's mansion and a cocktail reception for the press given by the Atlanta Women's Press Club at the Piedmont Driving Club. At the cocktail party, David Selznick finally met Margaret Mitchell. But when the producer began to discuss a sequel to the movie, Mitchell politely excused herself. Afterward, she was presented to Clark Gable.

The pressure of the crowd around her was so great that she took Gable by the arm and hustled him into a quiet room. There behind locked doors the petite author and the actor who played her hero chatted in private. Afterward, Gable mentioned that Margaret Mitchell was "the most fascinating woman I've ever met." The Atlanta festivities culminated that evening with the long-awaited event, the four-hour premiere of *GWTW*.

OLIVIA DE HAVILLAND
ALMOST MISSES THE BALL

On the evening of the Junior League Ball, Olivia de Havilland and Vivien Leigh were to leave together for the Atlanta Municipal Auditorium. But when de Havilland knocked on Leigh's door, there was no answer.

De Havilland then phoned Selznick's room, and no one was there either. With rising panic she phoned the front desk, and her worst suspicions were confirmed: Everyone had left for the ball without her.

She asked the desk clerk to order a cab. Sorry, he told her, all the cabs in the city were tied up with the ball. Now near hysterics, de Havilland ordered the clerk to call the police. Within minutes, a police van arrived at the hotel, de Havilland jumped in, and the van sped to the auditorium with the siren blasting.

When the van arrived at the auditorium, de Havilland jumped out and hurried into the building. She could hear the voice of the master of ceremonies over the public address system introducing her costars. She hurried into the hall and up the aisle frantically trying to figure out where she belonged.

Unfortunately, no one had clued in the emcee that de Havilland wasn't in her seat in her assigned box. "And now, Melanie Wilkes— Miss Olivia de Havilland," he said as the spotlight swung to de Havilland's empty box. The audience gasped in momentary confusion. "Here I am," de Havilland called from the aisle. She waved her arms, and the spotlight found her. It followed her as she made her way to her box amid laughter and much applause from the relieved audience.

THE PREMIERE OF *GWTW*

Crowds gathered early in front of Loew's Grand Theatre, which was illuminated by nine searchlights. People didn't have a chance of getting in to see the film; they were there to watch the stars. Four hundred Georgia National Guardsmen formed a human cordon to hold back the enthusiastic crowd of 12,000 that surged forward as each star arrived.

Gable's arrival caused some women to scream with joy and others to faint dead away. The premiere was covered by radio stations, and Gable made a gentlemanly request of the audience when it was his turn at the microphone: "Tonight I am here just as a spectator. I want to see *Gone With the Wind* the same as you do. This is Margaret Mitchell's night and the people of Atlanta's night. Allow me to see *Gone With the Wind* as a spectator."

In addition to the Hollywood stars, Jock Whitney was attending the premiere with his silver-spooned friends, including the Vanderbilts, Herbert Bayard Swope, Nelson Rockefeller, J.P. Morgan, and John Jacob Astor. Also attending were Atlanta's favorite citizens, Margaret Mitchell and her husband John Marsh.

ATLANTA JOURNAL-CONSTITUTION

THE NIGHT OF THE ATLANTA PREMIERE.

As the title swept across the screen and Max Steiner's music swelled through the theater, many in the audience gasped at the beauty of the Technicolor production. They followed Scarlett from her innocent days as a flirtatious belle through her beleaguered days in war-torn Atlanta. They cheered when Scarlett shot the Yankee deserter and gripped their seats as she fended off the Shantytown attacker. By the end of the movie, as Melanie lay dying, many openly sobbed into handkerchiefs.

When the heavy curtains swept across the stage, the audience stood and broke into wild applause for Selznick, his stars, and Margaret Mitchell. In the speeches that followed the premiere, Margaret Mitchell, for the first time, shared her feelings about the film. She thanked Selznick "on behalf of me and my poor Scarlett" for "the grand things these actors have done." Although emotionally drained, the audience renewed their ovations with new spirit and echoed Margaret Mitchell's sentiments. David Selznick, with tears in his eyes, basked in the unrestrained praise. The endless trouble and months of hard work were finally worth it.

OTHER "PREMIERES"

Following the Atlanta premiere, *GWTW* blew to New York City and hit the Big Apple with hurricane force. Simultaneous "premieres" were held on Tuesday, December 19 at the Astor Theatre and the Loew's

UPI/BETTMAN ARCHIVE

THE HOLLYWOOD PREMIERE: JOCK WHITNEY, IRENE SELZNICK, DE HAVILLAND, SELZNICK, LEIGH, AND LAURENCE OLIVIER.

Capitol Theatre. The opening night at the Capitol was covered by a new medium, television, which broadcast the arrival of stars and special guests to several hundred television sets in the area.

Most city newspapers sent reviewers to cover one or the other premiere, but the *New York Daily News* dispatched a reviewer to each theater. The next morning, the *Daily News* printed both four-star reviews. Wanda Hale, who had attended the premiere at the Astor, called the film "the most magnificent motion picture of all time." Kate Cameron, who saw the film at the Capitol, wrote, "There has never been a picture like David O. Selznick's *Gone With the Wind*."

The critic for *The New York Times*, Frank Nugent, wrote: "The greatest motion picture mural we have seen and the most ambitious film-making venture in Hollywood's spectacular history." The *Post*'s Archer Winsten noted: "Just as *Birth of a Nation* was a milestone of movie history, *Gone With the Wind* represents a supreme effort."

The next major premiere for *GWTW* took place in Los Angeles on Thursday, December 28 at the Fox Carthay Circle. This most glamorous premiere of all was held three days before the deadline set by the Academy of Motion Picture Arts and Sciences for films to qualify for 1939's Academy Awards. And all of Hollywood's glitterati attended, including *GWTW*'s cast, the unsuccessful contenders, Selznick's detractors, and his well-wishers, too. Selznick was enjoying the pinnacle of his success.

SELZNICK'S SEQUEL IDEAS

Almost as soon as the previews were over, Selznick started seriously thinking about a sequel to *GWTW*. He asked Kay Brown to approach Margaret Mitchell about writing the further adventures of Scarlett and Rhett or selling the rights to the characters. Mitchell, though, refused to consider either possibility.

But Selznick was undaunted and wrote to Brown: "If we can't get a sequel I would still be delighted to have a story to be called *The Daughter of Scarlett O'Hara*, with Vivien playing the daughter. Don't you think we might persuade Mitchell to write such a story as a novel, or a novelette, or even as a short story?

"I realize that we killed off Bonnie Blue, and it is not clear to me as to how Scarlett would get herself pregnant again, but then Scarlett, after all, was Scarlett, and there must have been other men in her life after Rhett walked out the door. Maybe we could talk about a marriage beyond Rhett, or perhaps even have an opening sequence in the story and in the picture dealing with her fourth husband."

Margaret Mitchell turned down that idea as well, and Selznick gave up hope of reprising the story of Scarlett O'Hara.

HOW *GWTW* CHANGED THE OSCAR PRESENTATIONS FOREVER

February 29, 1940, 8:30 P.M. The place: the Coconut Grove of the Ambassador Hotel in Los Angeles. The event: the twelfth annual awards presentation of the Academy of Motion Picture Arts and Sciences.

Hollywood was abuzz and aglitter with Oscar fever that afternoon. As was the custom, the names of the Oscar winners were revealed in advance to the press with newspapers making a solemn promise not to break the news before the ceremonies. But one newspaper couldn't contain the excitement.

The *Los Angeles Times* printed the names of the winners and splashed *Gone With the Wind* in banner headlines across the front page. The results greeted Academy Award goers as they arrived for the banquet and prompted the Academy to initiate a protocol for future Award presentations.

Since then, the names of the winners have been sealed in envelopes by Price, Waterhouse and Company, a firm of certified public accountants. This ensures that the results are, indeed, kept secret until the presenter says "And the winner is . . . "

1939 ACADEMY AWARDS: "THE WINNERS ARE . . ."

Gone With the Wind, Best Picture

GWTW took top honors in a resplendent field that included *Dark Victory*, *Goodbye, Mr. Chips*, *Love Affair*, *Mr. Smith Goes to Washington*, *Ninotchka*, *Of Mice and Men*, *Stagecoach*, *The Wizard of Oz*, and *Wuthering Heights*.

Vivien Leigh, Best Actress, Gone With the Wind

Spencer Tracy presented the Oscar for Best Actress to Vivien Leigh for her portrayal of Scarlett O'Hara. The other nominees included Greer Garson (*Goodbye, Mr. Chips*), Bette Davis (*Dark Victory*), Irene Dunne (*Love Affair*), and Greta Garbo (*Ninotchka*).

Robert Donat, Best Actor, *Goodbye, Mr. Chips*

Clark Gable as Rhett Butler lost the Best Actor Award to Robert Donat's touching portrayal of schoolteacher Mr. Chips. The other contenders were Laurence Olivier (*Wuthering Heights*), James Stewart (*Mr. Smith Goes to Washington*), and Mickey Rooney (*Babes in Arms*).

Hattie McDaniel, Best Supporting Actress, *Gone With the Wind*

Her performance as Mammy earned the Best Supporting Actress Award for Hattie McDaniel, the first black performer to win an Oscar. She was up against Olivia de Havilland (*Gone With the Wind*), Geraldine Fitzgerald (*Wuthering Heights*), Edna May Oliver (*Drums Along the Mohawk*), and Maria Ouspenskaya (*Love Affair*).

Thomas Mitchell, Best Supporting Actor, *Stagecoach*

Thomas Mitchell was nominated in this category for his role in *Stagecoach*, not for his portrayal of *GWTW*'s Gerald O'Hara or for his work in *Mr. Smith Goes to Washington*. But with such heavyweights in his corner, he was a predicted winner. His competition included Brian Aherne (*Juarez*), Brian Donlevy (*Beau Geste*), and double nominations from *Mr. Smith Goes to Washington*—Claude Rains and Harry Carey. Curiously, Leslie Howard's portrayal of Ashley Wilkes was bypassed as a nomination for Best Supporting Actor.

Victor Fleming, Best Director, *Gone With the Wind*

Although Victor Fleming was one of three directors to work on *GWTW*, he received sole on-screen credit and garnered the Academy Award for Best Director. Among his competition were Frank Capra (*Mr. Smith Goes to Washington*), John Ford (*Stagecoach*), Sam Wood (*Goodbye, Mr. Chips*), and William Wyler (*Wuthering Heights*).

Other Academy Awards for *GWTW* included Sidney Howard, Best Screenplay; Ernest Haller and Ray Rennahan, Best Photography; Lyle Wheeler, Best Art Direction; and Hal C. Kern and James E. Newcom, Best Film Editing. David O. Selznick received the Irving G. Thalberg Memorial Award "for the most consistent high quality of production

UPI/BETTMAN ARCHIVE

HATTIE MCDANIEL ON OSCAR NIGHT
WITH ACTRESS FAY BAINTER.

during 1939." A special plaque went to William Cameron Menzies "for outstanding achievement in the use of color for the enhancement of dramatic mood in the production *Gone With the Wind.*"

With an unprecedented thirteen nominations in twelve categories (double nomination for Best Supporting Actress), *GWTW* might have swept the Academy Awards. But the film did not win in every nomination category. In addition to Gable's loss of the Best Actor Award, Jack Cosgrove lost the Best Special Effects Award to *The Rains Came*; Max Steiner lost the Best Musical Score Award to *The Wizard of Oz*; and Thomas Moulton lost the Best Sound Recording Award to *When Tomorrow Comes*. However, by the end of the Oscar presentations, *GWTW* had won a record-breaking eight Academy Awards.

TIDBITS FROM OSCAR NIGHT

• Bob Hope made his first appearance as Oscar's master of ceremonies. Walter Wanger, the new president of the Academy, introduced Hope as the "Rhett Butler of the airwaves." Hope commented to the audience, "What a wonderful thing, this benefit for David Selznick."

• Sidney Howard's win for Best Screenplay made him the first posthumous Academy Award winner.

• Hattie McDaniel's win for Best Supporting Actress made her the first black performer to win an Oscar. She was also the first black performer to attend the Academy Awards banquet.

When McDaniel's name was announced, she whooped a "Hallelujah," rushed to the podium, and began her acceptance speech. Soon she was so overcome by tears, she sobbed a quiet "thank you" and hurried back to her table. There she buried her face in her hands and cried. Olivia de Havilland, who had lost to McDaniel, went to offer her congratulations. Then, feeling overcome by her own disappointment, de Havilland left the room and burst into tears herself.

• Spencer Tracy, the presenter of the Oscars for Best Actor and Actress, had left a hospital bed where he was suffering from strep throat to attend the Awards ceremony.

• After the ceremony, David Selznick sat silent and sullen as he rode to a post-Oscar party with his publicity director, Russell Birdwell. Suddenly Selznick turned on Birdwell. "I don't know why we didn't get the best-actor award for Gable. Somewhere you failed. You didn't put on the proper campaign; otherwise, Clark would have been sure to get it." Birdwell was stunned, especially because of all the Oscars *GWTW* did get. When Birdwell didn't show up at work for two days, Selznick phoned him and apologized. "I was a pig. I worked so hard and waited so long, I got piggish and wanted everything."

• Gable, too, was disappointed about not having won an Oscar for Rhett Butler. On the way home from the Academy Award ceremony, his actress-wife Carole Lombard tried to snap her husband out of his bad mood. "Aw, don't be blue, Pappy. I just know we'll bring one home next year." "No, we won't," Gable said dejectedly. "This was it. This was my last chance." Lombard was furious: "Not you, you self-centered bastard! I mean me!"

GWTW CAPTURES OTHER HONORS

• In December 1939, the New York Film Critics voted Vivien Leigh their Best Actress. Victor Fleming ranked third in the Critics' Best Director category.

• The *Photoplay* Magazine Gold Medal Award was the only one granted on the basis of balloting by the moviegoing public. In 1939, this oldest industry award was bestowed upon David O. Selznick for *GWTW* as "the best photoplay of the year."

• The National Board of Review Awards published an annual listing of the ten best movies. Voting was done by a Committee on Exceptional Films, and in 1940, the National Board ranked *GWTW* ninth on its top ten list. Number One was *The Grapes of Wrath*, and Number Ten was *Rebecca*.

• The *Film Daily* annually polled movie critics across the country and compiled a list of the ten best films. *GWTW* was included in the 1941 poll because the film was then in general release. Of the 548 ballots cast, 452 were enough to declare *GWTW* the first-place winner.

• In 1977, the *Photoplay* Gold Medal Award went to *GWTW* as the "all-time favorite movie."

• In 1977, the American Film Institute named *GWTW* "America's Greatest Movie" as the result of a poll of its 350,000 members. The announcement was made at a gala benefit at the Kennedy Center's Opera House.

• In 1987, the Hollywood Centennial Committee of the Hollywood Chamber of Commerce announced results of a survey of major U.S. film critics, professors of film, and subscribers to the journal *Film and History*.

The survey, conducted by Siena College Research Institute in upstate New York, included the following rating of the greatest American films:

1. *Citizen Kane*
2. *Gone With the Wind*
3. *Casablanca*
4. *It's a Wonderful Life*
5. *On the Waterfront*
6. *Searchers*
7. *The Godfather*
8. *The Birth of a Nation*
9. *The Wizard of Oz*
10. *City Lights*

EVERYONE WANTS TO SEE *GWTW*

During the film's first run, theaters showed *GWTW* either three times a day with unreserved seating or twice a day with reserved seating. Selznick was in favor of reserved seats because this eliminated long lines of patrons waiting outside the theater for the next showing. Generally, patrons paid 75 cents for a matinee ticket, while evening showings cost $1. Evening loge seating was $1.50. Regular movie tickets at this time were usually around 25 cents and rarely cost more than 50 cents.

Despite the high admission prices, everyone wanted to see *GWTW*. By Christmas 1939, the movie had grossed nearly one million dollars. When its phenomenal first run ended in June 1940, *GWTW* had earned nearly $24 million. And more than 25 million people in the United States had been overcome by Scarlett fever.

THE PHENOMENON OF *GWTW* BEGINS

Although most films had a short first-run life of several weeks, Selznick believed he could hold the public's interest in *GWTW* for at least two years with careful planning.

When *GWTW*'s first run ended in June 1940, MGM and Selznick International took the film out of circulation. To whet the appetites of those who hadn't been able to afford the premium prices of the film's initial run, print ads promised that *GWTW* would return the following year at reduced admissions.

To kick off the popular-priced engagements, MGM planned a First Anniversary Premiere bash in Atlanta for December 12, 1940. Another talent search was arranged, not for a new Scarlett, but for a Georgian miss to preside over the celebration. Louella Stone of Atlanta was chosen Miss Anniversary.

The top of the Loew's Grand Theatre was decorated with a replica of a three-tiered birthday cake complete with one sparkling candle. Guests paid $2.50 a ticket (which benefited the British War Relief Society) to see the film and to greet Vivien Leigh, Laurence Olivier, and Alfred Hitchcock, who were to make special appearances. Unfortunately, bad weather delayed the arrival of the celebrities until the following day.

Moviegoers were ecstatic when GWTW's general release began. Print ads shouted "Nothing cut but the price!" Twenty-four million people flocked to large cinemas in major cities as well as to small neighborhood theaters to see Scarlett battle hunger and despair. Matinee tickets sold for 40 cents, while evening tickets cost 55 cents. GWTW's second release not only earned $5 million but made the film the number-one box-office draw for 1941.

At the end of the 1941 general release, MGM decided to withdraw GWTW again. The prints were battered, but the studio believed one final fling for GWTW was possible. The film returned to movie theaters for the third time in the spring of 1942 and stayed in release until late 1943.

When MGM finally pulled the film from exhibition, all worn-out prints were destroyed, and GWTW was at last declared out of circulation. MGM, which by then had sole ownership of the film, announced that GWTW had grossed over $32 million. But the phenomenon was only beginning.

GWTW IS A HIT OVERSEAS

GWTW was not just an American phenomenon. The Wind swept overseas as well:

• In 1940 GWTW opened at the Ritz Theatre in war-torn London where the film played for 232 consecutive weeks, nearly four and a half years. This was the longest film run in history.

• Adolf Hitler apparently was smitten with GWTW's saucy heroine and her damn-Yankee attitude. But when der Führer learned that GWTW was a source of encouragement to the underground resistance, he banned both the novel and the film from all German-occupied countries.

A GERMAN PROGRAM FOR *GWTW*.

• In the postwar years, *GWTW*'s message of survival spoke to thousands of newly liberated people who crammed European theaters to see Scarlett O'Hara triumph over her oppressors.

• *GWTW* debuted in West Berlin in 1954 and played for two and a half years. By the time four prints of the film had bit the dust, over 600,000 people had viewed the movie.

NOT EVERYONE LOVED *GWTW*

The Catholic Church's Legion of Decency gave *GWTW* a "B" rating, which meant the film was "morally objectionable in part for all." The Legion did not approve of "the low moral character, principles, and behavior of the main figures as depicted in the film; suggestive implications; the attractive portrayal of the immoral character of a supporting role in the story." (Belle Watling, perhaps?)

Usually such forceful censure of a film was enough to keep crowds away from the movie house, but not so with *GWTW*. Many saw the film despite the objections of their church.

GWTW MERCHANDISING MANIA

Not only were millions of people seeing *GWTW*, they were also buying hundreds of products with *GWTW* tie-ins:

• La Cross promoted three shades of nail polish—Scarlett O'Hara Morning, Noon, and Night—with this warning: "Scarlett O'Hara Danger! ... Wear it for romance. ... A nail polish so glamorous you'll want to live up to it. ... Sirenizing deep red to add Scarlett glamour like a jewel."

• The Rhett Butler bow by Slim Jim Bows was inspired by the cravats worn by Clark Gable in the film.

• A series of Scarlett O'Hara dolls was popular. The dolls wore costumes reminiscent of various scenes in the movie.

• A Chinese checkers–type game called Bet Chu Can't was sold as "The Scarlett O'Hara game."

• A simulated cameo brooch, designed to resemble the one worn by Vivien Leigh, was offered for fifteen cents and three wrappers from Lux toilet soap.

• Nunnally's, "The Candy of the South," packaged a box of Scarlett chocolates. The box looked like a book, had a photograph of Vivien Leigh on the cover, and contained candy pieces named after the film's characters: Scarlett Fantasies, Rhett Caramels, Melanie Molasses Strings, Tara Pecans, Ashley Brazils, Tarleton Strawberries, Prissy Peppermints, and Gerald O'Hara Almonds.

• The "Scarlett O'Hara Morning Gory" was awarded a gold medal from the All American Seed Selection Society.

• There were hundreds of other merchandising tie-ins authorized by Loew's, Inc. Among them were Scarlett and Rhett wristwatches and statuettes; Scarlett O'Hara perfume, perfume decanters, and dress patterns; *GWTW* fashions including costumes, handkerchiefs, scarves, snoods, turbans, hats, and veils. Fashions for the home included living-room furniture, *GWTW* quilts, slipcovers, and drapery valences. There were *GWTW* leather products, and for kids, *GWTW* paper dolls and paint boxes.

In honor of the film, the Southern Comfort Corporation debuted two new potent potables:

Scarlett O'Hara Cocktail

juice of ¼ fresh lime
1 jigger cranberry juice
1 jigger Southern Comfort

Combine the ingredients in a cocktail shaker filled with cracked ice. Shake well, and strain into a cocktail glass.

Rhett Butler Cocktail

juice of ½ lime
juice of ⅛ lemon
½ teaspoon sugar
1 barspoon Curacao
1 jigger Southern Comfort

Combine ingredients in a cocktail shaker filled with cracked ice. Shake well, and strain into a cocktail glass.

The slogan for the new cocktails was "no more than two lest you be *Gone With the Wind.*" The American public immediately took to the cocktail named after its favorite heroine, and the drink remains popular today. But what about the Rhett Butler Cocktail? The drink never achieved popularity, and it disappeared from the scene as quickly as its namesake left for Charleston at the end of the film.

COOKING UP A STORM
WITH THE *GWTW COOKBOOK*

Purchasers of Pebeco toothpaste received an unparalleled premium: *THE GONE WITH THE WIND Cookbook*. The forty-eight-page cookbook

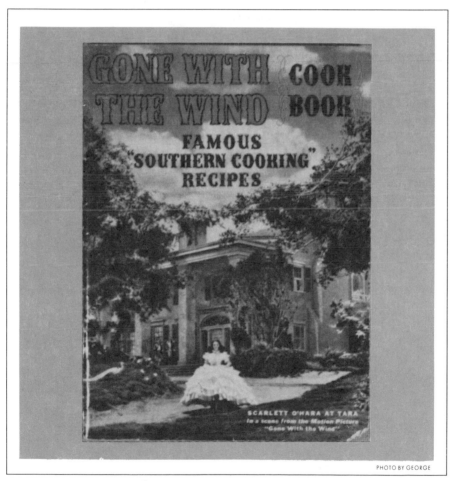

PHOTO BY GEORGE

 THE *GWTW COOKBOOK*.

presented suggestions for *GWTW* parties as well as 128 "famous Southern cooking recipes" from soup to nuts. Included were

> Southland Vegetable Soup
> Gerald O'Hara Ham Steak
> Tara Supper Deviled Crabs
> Tarleton Twins' Broiled Oysters
>   On the Half Shell
> Mammy's Creole Rice
> Plantation Corn Omelet
> Atlanta Waffles
> Twelve Oaks Plum Pudding
> Aunt Pittypat's Coconut Pudding
> Georgia Peach Trifle
> Melanie's Sweet Potato Pie

There was no mention of recipes for Ashley Artichokes or Rhett Butler Rutabagas. You're on your own with those.

GWTW IS AN INSPIRATION

• *Kiss the Boys Goodbye* by Clare Boothe opened on Broadway in September 1938 and told the story of an Alabama beauty who longs for Hollywood and the chance to play Velvet O'Toole. The play became a film in 1941.

• In *Strike Up the Band*, Mickey Rooney and Judy Garland sang the praises of Scarlett and Rhett in "Our Love Affair."

• The 1940 Broadway musical revue *Keep Off the Grass* featured a hilarious *GWTW* takeoff with Ilka Chase playing Scarlett, Ray Bolger as Ashley, and Jimmy Durante in the role of Rhett Butler.

• The film *Let's Go Slap Happy* was billed as "the dizziest, dopiest, daffiest burlesque on *Gone With the Wind*." Ben Goman starred as "Harlette O'Hare" opposite Tommy Reilly who played "Rat Butler."

• Cecil B. DeMille's 1941 film *Reap the Wild Wind* teamed Paulette Goddard (with a Southern accent), Louise Beavers as Mammy, Hedda Hopper as a swooning aunt, and Oscar Polk (*GWTW*'s Pork) as house servant "Salt Meat" in a merry Technicolor romp that included various and sundry disasters.

GWTW IS SOLD

By April 1942 the huge profits from *GWTW* were pouring into Selznick International. On the advice of tax lawyers who feared that most of the profits would go toward taxes, Selznick was advised to dissolve Selznick International Pictures and to sell his interest in *GWTW*.

Selznick was reluctant to let go of his share of the film. But the attorneys advised that unless he did so, the capital-gains strategy they had worked out with the government might be challenged. Besides, they argued, the public would soon grow tired of *GWTW*, and there couldn't be more than another million dollars in profits to be made. So Selznick decided to sell his interest in the film to Jock Whitney for $400,000 and to dissolve the company. (Selznick subsequently formed another film company.) Whitney then sold his interest in *GWTW* for $2.4 million to MGM, the ultimate triumph for Louis B. Mayer.

With their respective windfalls from the sales, Selznick and Whitney sent a check for $50,000 to Margaret Mitchell to show their gratitude to the Atlanta author. This brought the total amount she received for the movie rights to $100,000.

Postscript: When *GWTW* was re-released in mid-1947 and played through 1948, the film brought in $9 million. When Selznick learned about the profits he missed out on, he became enraged: "I could strangle [the tax lawyers] with my bare hands in cold blood."

WITH A GUST, *THE WIND* RETURNS

Americans had not seen *GWTW* since November 1943 when MGM put the film into mothballs after its successful third reissue. However, fans wanted to know when it would reappear.

They wrote letters to Selznick asking when the film would be shown again. Selznick received a petition signed by every student of Western State High School in Kalamazoo, Michigan requesting to see the "supreme film" one more time. Even Margaret Mitchell took pen in hand: "So many children who were not old enough to see it when it was last here have requested that I ask you when it will be back. So I am asking for them, and because I'd like to see it myself." Selznick passed all the mail on to MGM, which decided to bring *GWTW* back to the theaters in June 1947.

MGM splurged on the 1947 revival of *GWTW*. There were new Technicolor prints and a spanking new ad campaign. Posters for the film for the first time showed Rhett holding Scarlett in his arms and boasted that "Everybody wants to see *Gone With the Wind.*"

And everybody did. Crowds this time around rivaled those that had waited on line for tickets in 1939. Many who saw the film during its first release returned to see if the film was as good as they remembered it. They brought their children, too, to introduce a new generation to the story of Scarlett and Rhett.

In Atlanta alone, records for popular-price admission were shattered. Thousands stood in double lines at Loew's Grand Theatre on the first day of *GWTW*'s return. Some fans, eager for tickets, stood in line at the box office as early as 8 A.M. to make sure they saw the film. When *GWTW*'s fourth reissue run ended in late 1948, the film had earned $9.1 million.

THE STARS SHINE ON

◆

THE AFTER-THE-MOVIE LIVES
OF *GWTW'S* STARS

Leslie Howard

After he completed work on *Intermezzo*, Leslie Howard sailed to England. He began his own filmmaking company so he would finally be able to realize his dream of directing. He immersed himself in directing *Pimpernel Smith* and *The First of the Few*.

England was at war. Howard undertook a lecture tour on behalf of the British Council and traveled to Spain and Portugal where he spoke in various cities about the theater. Spain was still neutral, and it was whispered even then that Howard was really on a secret mission for the British government. But this was never confirmed.

On June 1, 1943, Howard, at the end of his tour, boarded a commercial airplane in Lisbon, Portugal bound for England. In a tragic coincidence, Prime Minister Winston Churchill was at the same time flying back to England on another plane after attending a military meeting.

At 12:45 P.M., as Howard's plane crossed the Bay of Biscay, the pilot sighted the approach of eight German fighter planes. Whether the Germans believed that Churchill was on the plane or whether they mistook the craft for Churchill's is not known. But in the next few seconds, the fighters opened fire on the unarmed civilian aircraft. The plane exploded into flames and crashed into the sea. All aboard, including 53-year-old Leslie Howard, were killed.

Clark Gable

Relieved that *GWTW* was finished, Gable returned to work at MGM and life with Carole Lombard. But their idyllic happiness was shattered when the Japanese bombs found their targets at Pearl Harbor.

Lombard, a dyed-in-the-wool patriot, agreed to help in the war effort by traveling to her home state of Indiana on a bond-selling tour. The tour was wildly successful. In Indianapolis alone, Lombard sold over $2 million in defense bonds. She was on her way home to Gable on January 16, 1942 when, a few minutes after taking off from Las Vegas, her plane smashed headlong into Mount Potosi. Lombard and everyone else on the plane, including her mother and MGM's publicity man Otto Winkler, were killed instantly.

Lombard's death devastated Clark Gable. Despite the objections of his studio, he enlisted in the Army Air Force. He flew in bombing missions over Germany during his two-year tour of duty and was discharged with the rank of major.

When Gable returned home from the war, he returned to the only life he knew: making movies. MGM teamed him with young actresses such as Greer Garson, Ava Gardner, and Grace Kelly, and Gable recaptured his success in films such as *Adventure, Lone Star,* and *Mogambo.*

In 1954, at the height of his popularity, Gable left MGM over a contract dispute and began a freelance acting career. Gable had a lingering resentment toward MGM that he had never been offered a percentage of *GWTW*'s enormous profits. He was determined that future contracts would include percentage clauses.

In the area of love, Gable was less successful. He continually searched for a replacement for Carole Lombard and thought he had found her in an Englishwoman, Lady Sylvia Ashley. Their 1949 marriage, though, ended in divorce two years later. Gable had better luck in his fifth trip to the altar. In 1955, he married Kay Williams Spreckels and at last found the happiness that had eluded him since Lombard's death.

His film work now found him playing opposite actresses such as Susan Hayward, Jane Russell, and Eleanor Parker in films for various studios. In 1957 he starred in another story of the Old South, *Band of Angels* with Yvonne DeCarlo. *Variety* called Gable's character, a reformed slave trader, "reminiscent of Rhett Butler."

In 1960 Gable signed to star as an aging cowboy in Arthur Miller's *The Misfits.* He was teamed with Marilyn Monroe, Montgomery Clift, and Thelma Ritter in a story filmed on location in the scorching Nevada flats. Tensions on the set resulting from script problems and an unstable

Marilyn Monroe drove Gable to distraction, but he always remained the professional. He even insisted on doing his own stunt work for scenes, including a horse-roping sequence in which he was dragged 400 feet through an alkali bed.

Throughout the production, Gable stayed sane by looking ahead to the future. His wife was pregnant with their first child, and he was thrilled at the prospect of becoming a father. He was committed to making one more film after *The Misfits*, and then he planned to retire to raise his child—a son, he hoped.

But *The Misfits* took its toll. Shortly after filming ended, Gable suffered a heart attack. Ten days later on November 16, 1960 the King of Hollywood was dead at age 59. As a sad postscript, the child he always wanted but never saw—a son, John Clark Gable—was born four months later.

Vivien Leigh

After *GWTW*, Vivien Leigh's film career continued with her roles in *Waterloo Bridge* with Robert Taylor and in *That Hamilton Woman* with Laurence Olivier. In her personal life, Leigh was now starring as Mrs. Laurence Olivier, and the couple worked together in various stage and screen projects. She moved comfortably into the role of Lady Olivier when her husband was knighted in 1947.

Leigh was playing Sabina in Thornton Wilder's *The Skin of Our Teeth* when she was first diagnosed as having a tubercular patch on her lung. She ignored the seriousness of her condition and continued to smoke and drink excessively and to work to the point of exhaustion.

What she could not ignore were the periods of manic depression she suffered. During the depressive phase, she was depressed, had difficulty thinking and concentrating, and lost her appetite as well as her ability to sleep. In the manic phase, she became wild and lashed out at others for no reason. Her judgment was poor during these times, and she often was sexually indiscriminate. Frequently, only electroshock therapy could restore her mental stability.

In 1948 Leigh starred in the London production of *A Streetcar Named Desire*, produced and directed by Olivier. Leigh's outstanding portrayal of the fading Southern belle, Blanche DuBois, won her the role in the Warner Brothers film and subsequently her second Academy Award.

No matter where Leigh traveled, she was recognized as Scarlett O'Hara. Fans of *GWTW* packed theaters to see her in plays, shouted to her on the street, and hounded her for autographs at train stations, airports, and hotels. "Did Scarlett get Rhett back?" they always asked, and Leigh replied that she didn't think so. In 1960 the question became poignant on a personal level when Olivier, the love of her own life, asked for a divorce.

Leigh was crushed by the ending of her marriage and plunged herself into work as an antidote to the pain. She starred in the 1961 film *The Roman Spring of Mrs. Stone* and accepted a role in the 1963 Broadway musical, *Tovarich*. In the musical, Leigh sang and danced her way into the hearts of the critics, and her performance earned her a Tony Award.

After her stage triumph, Leigh was overcome by another cycle of manic depression. Her recuperation was slow, but she eventually felt well enough to undertake the role of a Southern woman in decline in the 1965 film *Ship of Fools*. For her performance, she received the French equivalent of the Oscar, the Étoile Crystal.

In 1967, fifty-four-year-old Leigh began rehearsals for the London production of Edward Albee's *A Delicate Balance*. But she was forced to withdraw from the play at the end of May. The tuberculosis that wracked her body was found to have spread to both lungs.

Leigh refused hospitalization. She chose instead to remain at home for the three months the doctors said it would take to recover from this latest and most serious bout of illness. Those three months were not hers to have.

Newspapers around the world that carried the news of her July 8 death sadly announced: "Scarlett O'Hara Is Dead." The evening after her death, in recognition of their loss, all the theaters in London's West End extinguished their lights for one hour to honor the memory of Vivien Leigh.

Olivia de Havilland

Warner Brothers loaned Olivia de Havilland to other studios after her appearance in *GWTW*. She played in *Raffles* for Samuel Goldwyn and in *Hold Back the Dawn* for Paramount. Although *Hold Back the Dawn* brought her a second Academy Award nomination, an Oscar remained tantalizingly out of reach.

Just as Jack Warner had predicted, de Havilland became dissatisfied with the projects the studio offered her. They tossed her a few bones that she enjoyed such as *Strawberry Blonde*, *The Male Animal*, and *In This Our Life* with Bette Davis. She was hungry, though, for a meaty role that could capture the elusive Oscar. When she refused to accept unsuitable parts, Warner suspended her without salary.

She endured seven such suspensions, and when her contract expired in 1943, de Havilland decided not to renew. But Warner had an ace up his sleeve. He ordered the nine months she had spent on suspension added to the end of her contract. By this time de Havilland had had it with Warner's dictatorial ways. She decided to take him to court.

She fought her case in three successive courtrooms until the Superior Court of California ruled that a seven-year contract ended after the seventh year. Warner was foiled but not for long; he initiated a squeeze play. He brought the case to the appellate court, then warned every Hollywood producer not to hire her since de Havilland was still his contract player.

When the dust of this fight finally settled nearly two years after it began, de Havilland was the winner. The appeals judge ruled that adding suspension time to her contract "would amount to virtual peonage." This precedent-setting decision for contract actors signaled the death knell for the powerful movie studio system.

Fresh from her legal victory, de Havilland accepted the role of an unwed mother fighting to regain custody of her child in Paramount's *To Each His Own* in 1946. Her heart-wrenching performance finally won the long-sought Academy Award as Best Actress. This was followed by her role in *The Snake Pit* in 1948, which earned a fourth Oscar nomination, and *The Heiress* in 1949, which captured her second Academy Award. The year proved to be a good one personally as well. Her 1946 union with Marcus Goodrich was blessed in 1949 with a son, Benjamin.

After 1951 de Havilland accepted roles on the stage, in films, and on television. Following the crumbling of her marriage, she found happiness again with Pierre Galante. They married in 1955, and de Havilland moved to France. They had a daughter, Giselle, in 1957. But the second marriage was fated to end as well; they were divorced in 1977.

De Havilland finds it ironic that she is the last of *GWTW*'s four stars since she was the only one to die in the film. Her career continues today. She played Henry Fonda's wife in *Roots: The Next Generation*. In 1986 she crossed to the other side of the Mason-Dixon line when she played Mrs. Neal, a Northerner and hospital administrator, in the twelve-hour miniseries *North and South, Book II*. That same year she starred with Rex Harrison and Amy Irving in the four-hour miniseries *Anastasia: The Mystery of Anna*.

WHATEVER HAPPENED TO . . .

Thomas Mitchell (Gerald O'Hara)

• Notable films following *GWTW*: *Our Town*, *This Above All*, *Tales of Manhattan*, *The Immortal Sergeant*, *The Sullivans*, *Wilson*, *The Keys of the Kingdom*, *The Outlaw*.

• Played with Clark Gable and Harry Davenport in *Adventure* and Olivia de Havilland in *The Dark Mirror*.

• Returned to the stage in 1950 as a replacement for Lee J. Cobb in *Death of a Salesman*.

• Entered the new medium of television and won an Emmy as Best Television Actor of 1952.

• Played in the film *High Noon* with Gary Cooper then headed back to Broadway for the 1953 musical *Hazel Flagg* (based on David O. Selznick's film *Nothing Sacred*). Mitchell won a Tony Award as Best Actor of the Year in a Musical.

• Continued his work in television with appearances in two series, *Mayor of the Town* and *Glencannon*, and in films. His last film was 1961's *Pocketful of Miracles*.

• Died of cancer on December 17, 1962.

Barbara O'Neil (Ellen O'Hara)

• Made ten films after *GWTW*, then headed to Broadway. Her stage appearances included roles in *The Searching Wind*, *Affairs of State*, and *Portrait of a Lady*.

• Continued her film work in *I Remember Mama*, *Whirlpool*, *Angel Face*, and *The Nun's Story*.

• Was artist-in-residence from 1958–1960 at the University of Denver.

• Returned to Broadway in 1960 for *Little Moon of Alban*.

• Retired from acting to live in Connecticut.

• Died on September 3, 1980.

Evelyn Keyes (Suellen O'Hara)

• Worked with Columbia Pictures for eight years and had roles in

Here Comes Mr. Jordan, Ladies in Retirement, A Thousand and One Nights, and *The Jolson Story.*

• Left Columbia to pursue film work on her own. Keyes captured roles in *Enchantment, Mrs. Mike, The Prowler, The Seven Year Itch,* and *Around the World in 80 Days.*

• Was married three times, to director Charles Vidor, director John Huston, and musician Artie Shaw.

• Starred with Don Ameche in the nationwide stage tour of *No, No, Nanette.*

• Became an author in 1971 with the novel *I Am a Billboard.* The book detailed the efforts of a Southern actress to make it big in Hollywood.

• Published her autobiography in 1976 entitled *Scarlett O'Hara's Younger Sister.*

Ann Rutherford (Carreen O'Hara)

• Notable films after *GWTW: Of Human Hearts, A Christmas Carol, Pride and Prejudice, The Secret Life of Walter Mitty, The Adventures of Don Juan, Orchestra Wives.*

• Married William Dozier in the 1950s (who was formerly married to Joan Fontaine), which made her stepmother to Olivia de Havilland's niece.

• Guest-starred in an episode of *Love American Style* in 1969 for ABC-TV.

• Appeared in *They Only Kill Their Masters* with June Allyson and Peter Lawford for MGM in 1972.

Hattie McDaniel (Mammy)

• Notable films after *GWTW: Since You Went Away, In This Our Life* (playing with Olivia de Havilland), Walt Disney's *Song of the South.*

• Continued to make radio appearances and entered the world of television with her character "Beulah," but her career was stopped by cancer.

• Died on October 26, 1952.

UPI/BETTMAN ARCHIVE

SCARLETT WITH MAMMIE (HATTIE MCDANIEL).

Butterfly McQueen (Prissy)

• Notable films after *GWTW*: *Cabin in the Sky* (playing with Eddie Anderson), *Mildred Pierce, Duel in the Sun*.

• Costarred in the early '50s with Ethel Waters in the television series *Beulah*.

• Appeared in the film *Amazing Grace* in 1974.

• Honored by the Black Filmmakers Hall of Fame in 1975.

• Played a fairy godmother in the 1978 ABC children's special, *The Seven Wishes of Joanna Peabody*.

• Costarred with Harrison Ford in 1986's *The Mosquito Coast*.

• Devotes her time to volunteer work in Harlem.

Laura Hope Crews (Aunt Pittypat)

• Accepted a role in Broadway's *Arsenic and Old Lace* but was stricken with a kidney ailment in October 1942.

• Died on November 13, 1942.

Eddie Anderson (Uncle Peter)

• Notable films after *GWTW*: *You Can't Take It With You, Kiss the Boys Goodbye, Cabin in the Sky*.

• Took his "Rochester" character from radio to television in the 1950s on *The Jack Benny Show*. His character remained a staple during the decade the show was on the air. He reprised the character for several Jack Benny specials.

• Appeared in *It's a Mad, Mad, Mad, Mad World* in 1963, then announced his retirement.

• Tried a comeback in 1972 with a nightclub act. As a result he was signed for a role in Broadway's *Good News*. Ill health forced him to withdraw from rehearsals.

• Was honored by the Black Filmmakers Hall of Fame in 1975.

• Died on February 28, 1977.

Harry Davenport (Dr. Meade)

• Notable films after *GWTW*: *Meet Me in St. Louis, The Enchanted Forest, All This, and Heaven Too, Princess O'Rourke, Government Girl, Adventure.*

• Was active professionally right up to his death on August 9, 1949; his acting career spanned seventy-eight years.

Ona Munson (Belle Watling)

• Found herself typecast by the role of Belle Watling for the remainder of her career in films such as *Lady from Louisiana* and *The Cheaters*.

• Played Madame Gin Sling in *The Shanghai Gesture*, but the film and her performance were panned by the critics.

• Suffered from depression and ended her life with an overdose of barbiturates on February 11, 1955.

Carroll Nye (Frank Kennedy)

• The comeback that he envisioned for himself after *GWTW* eluded him.

• Abandoned his acting career to become the radio editor at the *Los Angeles Times*.

• Branched out into positions in radio broadcasting, public relations, and television.

• Died on March 17, 1974.

Victor Jory (Jonas Wilkerson)

• Notable films after *GWTW*: *A Midsummer Night's Dream*, *The Miracle Worker*, *The Fugitive Kind*, two Hopalong Cassidy films, *Papillon*, and *The Mountain Men*.

• Played in the 1959–1960 television series *Manhunt*.

• Recorded the narration for Atlanta's Cyclorama in 1967.

• Directed *On Golden Pond* and starred in *The Time of Your Life* for the Actors Theater of Louisville, Kentucky.

• Died on February 12, 1982.

George Reeves (Stuart Tarleton)

• Notable films after *GWTW*: *Lydia*, *So Proudly We Hail*, *Winged Victory*.

• Found success as Superman in the 1950s television series.

• Felt he was typecast as the Man of Steel and in despair he turned a gun on himself and ended his life on June 16, 1959.

Ward Bond (Tom, a Yankee Captain)

• Played in *The Maltese Falcon*, *Sergeant York*, *The Sullivans*, *It's a Wonderful Life*, *It Happened One Night* (with Clark Gable), *A Guy Named Joe*, *Joan of Arc*, and *Made for Each Other* as well as in seventeen John Wayne films.

• Moved into television where, from 1957 to 1960, he starred as the wagon master on the series *Wagon Train*.

• Died on November 5, 1960.

Rand Brooks (Charles Hamilton)

• Played in *The Old Maid*, *Babes in Arms*, *Cheers for Miss Bishop*, *Lady in the Dark*, *Joan of Arc*.

• Played Hopalong Cassidy's sidekick in the western film series.

• Was Marilyn Monroe's first leading man in *Ladies of the Chorus* in 1948.

• Married comedian Stan Laurel's daughter, Lois.

• Returned to the screen in the '60s for two westerns, *Stagecoach to Danger's Rock* and *Comanche Station*.

• Abandoned his acting career for a quiet life in California.

Jane Darwell (Dolly Merriwether)

• Among her 150-plus credits were roles in *Rose of the Rancho, The Oxbow Incident, Caged,* and six Shirley Temple movies.

• Won an Academy Award for her portrayal of Ma Joad in *The Grapes of Wrath.*

• Appeared last in the "Feed the Birds" sequence in Walt Disney's 1964 film *Mary Poppins.*

• Died on August 13, 1967.

SEE WHAT A SMALL PART CAN DO FOR YOU

Isabel Jewell, who played Emmy Slattery, had only one scene in the second part of the film (when she and husband Jonas Wilkerson pay a call at Tara) and only one line of dialogue ("Yes, it's me"). The role just seemed larger because of the talk about Emmy's white trash ways in Part One of the movie.

The Wyoming-born actress was destined for small roles. Her pre-*GWTW* work included roles as the seamstress who accompanies Ronald Colman to the guillotine in *Tale of Two Cities* in 1935 and as a lady of the evening in 1937's *Lost Horizon.* Her later film work included supporting parts in *Northwest Passage, High Sierra,* and *The Snake Pit.* Her career declined in the late 1950s.

Jewell had hard times in her personal life as well. She ran afoul of the law in 1959 when she was arrested for passing bad checks in Las Vegas. In 1961 she was arrested for drunk driving and sentenced to a five-day jail term and a year's probation. She died on April 5, 1972.

Most of **Mary Anderson's** portrayal of Maybelle Merriwether ended up on the cutting-room floor. She is seen blushing briefly as her escort bids for her at the Atlanta Bazaar. But her screen career was launched with her *GWTW* appearance. She found roles in *All This, and Heaven Too* and *Cheers for Miss Bishop.* Her part in Broadway's *Guest in the House* led to a contract with Twentieth Century-Fox and impressive roles in *Lifeboat, The Song of Bernadette,* and *Wilson.* She later shared screen credits with Olivia de Havilland in *To Each His Own,* for which Anderson is best remembered. The Alabama native turned to television in the 1960s for the role of Catherine Harrington in the series *Peyton Place.*

Marjorie Reynolds's part as a guest at Twelve Oaks was so small she was seen coming down the staircase with Melanie and India but said her one line of dialogue off camera. Larger roles awaited her, though, such as playing opposite Bing Crosby and Fred Astaire in *Holiday Inn*. Her other films included *Star Spangled Rhythm*, *Dixie*, *Duffy's Tavern*, *Ministry of Fear*, *That Midnight Kiss*, and *Home Town Story*. But Idaho-born Reynolds found greater fame in television. In 1953 she began a five-year stint playing Peg Riley opposite William Bendix in *The Life of Riley*.

Cliff Edwards played a Reminiscent Soldier in the Shadow Scene in the Atlanta church-turned-hospital. Audiences never saw him; they only heard his sad story. The Missouri native sang and played the ukelele in vaudeville and then began his film career at MGM. He is best known for his recording of "Ja Da" and for "Singin' in the Rain," which he performed in *The Hollywood Revue of 1929*. His other film credits include *So This Is College*, *Saratoga* (in this film he got to sing with Clark Gable and Hattie McDaniel), *Maisie*, and *His Girl Friday*. But his best-remembered role was actually a very famous voice. He was the voice of Jiminy Cricket in Walt Disney's *Pinocchio*. During that film Edwards sang, "When You Wish Upon a Star," which won an Academy Award in 1940. Edwards died on July 17, 1971.

EPILOGUE:
MARGARET MITCHELL

"I have been writing since I was five-and-a-half years old, and until I got so busy cleaning up after *Gone with the Wind*, I always had something going." Now that the Atlanta premiere and the Academy Award presentations were over, Margaret again yearned to get "something going." But circumstances intervened.

With the world at war, Margaret spent her days working with Atlanta's Civilian Defense and the Red Cross. She sold war bonds, wrote letters to servicemen, and served as hostess and seamstress at Army canteens. In September 1941 Margaret traveled to Kearney, New Jersey to christen a new cruiser, the U.S.S. *Atlanta*.

Margaret kept busy fighting personal battles as well. Her ill and hospitalized father, Eugene Mitchell, depended on Margaret for his care until his death in 1944. Her novel also needed tending to: Margaret had to keep on top of the authorized foreign translations of *GWTW* as well as the pirated editions printed by unscrupulous publishers around the world.

On the home front, Macmillan published a "Victory" edition of *GWTW* on August 25, 1942. This hardcover volume was a sized-down version of the original and was printed on a cheaper grade of paper because of the wartime paper shortage. The dust jacket proudly carried the liberty insignia, which urged citizens to buy war bonds and stamps. First-year sales of the book, which retailed for $1.49, climbed to 23,572 copies, and an additional 42,450 copies sold from 1943 to 1944. During the last year of the war, sales mounted to 56,710 copies.

Margaret hoped to return to her typewriter after the war ended. But her husband, John Marsh, suffered a heart attack that nearly killed him in December 1945. His subsequent care took most of Margaret's time for over a year. He retired from his position at the Georgia Power Company in September 1947 and assumed much of the foreign *GWTW* business that Margaret had been handling on her own. As she wrote to a friend, "The work seems to get heavier and heavier as time goes on instead of getting lighter, and any hope of ever having an opportunity to do more writing is something I never even think about."

The early months of 1949 finally afforded Margaret some breathing space. Business pressures were easing, and Margaret had time to think about a new writing project. Maybe a continuation of Atlanta's history up to World War I? A play perhaps? Margaret toyed with the idea of a drama concerning a woman who writes a wildly successful book. But Margaret was sure of one thing: She would not write a sequel to *GWTW*. For her, the story of Scarlett and Rhett ended just as she had written it.

With hopes stirring for the beginning of a new work, Margaret and John endured the stifling early days of an Atlanta August. The fiery heat of Thursday, August 11 gave way to a cool evening breeze. Margaret had felt ill all day and thought that a night at the movies would be a welcome treat. She and John decided to see *A Canterbury Tale* at the Arts Theatre on Peachtree Street.

Margaret parked their car across from the theater and with John at her side began to cross the street. As they were halfway across, a speeding car rounded the curved street and headed straight for the couple. John hurried forward, but Margaret for some reason retreated backward. Brakes squealed. The car skidded and swerved into Margaret. She never made it back to the curb. The man behind the wheel, an off-duty taxi driver, admitted he had been drinking that afternoon.

Unconscious and terribly injured, Margaret was rushed to Atlanta's

Henry Grady Memorial Hospital. Doctors determined that her most serious injuries were a fractured skull and pelvis.

Crowds began gathering outside the hospital waiting for news about the forty-eight-year-old author. The hospital's switchboard was deluged with calls from all over the country. Radio news programs supplied hourly bulletins about her deteriorating condition. Margaret lingered for five days, and then her struggles ended. On August 16 radio stations announced the sad news of her death by playing "Tara's Theme."

AMERICA REMEMBERS MARGARET MITCHELL

Personal messages of condolence flooded Atlanta. President Harry S. Truman wired John Marsh on August 17: "The nation to which she brought international fame through a creative work of lasting merit shares the sorrow which has come to you with such sudden and tragic force. Great as an artist who gave the world an eternal book, the author of *Gone with the Wind* will also be remembered as a great soul who exemplified in her all-too-brief span of years the highest ideals of American womanhood."

Tributes appeared in newspapers across the nation and around the world. The *New York Times* wrote: "The South and the Nation have lost one of their most beloved and admired personages. Certainly she will always be one of our most remarkable literary figures." The *Charleston News and Courier* said that Margaret was "a dear, sweet woman who had the charity that vaunteth not itself. Her life and her book were the realization of genius, goodness, and modesty."

Sorrow over Margaret's death was quickly replaced with anger when it was revealed that the man who had run her down, Hugh D. Gravitt, had a string of arrests and convictions for traffic violations. When he was brought to trial two months after Margaret's death, he was convicted of criminally reckless driving and handed an eighteen-month jail sentence.

An outpouring of public sentiment screamed for safer driving. The Boy Scouts and Girl Scouts combined forces to promote a "Margaret Mitchell Minute" for the first anniversary of her death. Americans were urged to spend sixty seconds of silence remembering the author of *GWTW* and how suddenly a careless driver can take a life. The National Safety Council used the tragedy of Margaret's death in their campaigns.

The Atlanta traffic safety board renamed itself the Margaret Mitchell Safety Council in honor of the city's most famous citizen. (It has since become the Georgia Safety Council.) Margaret was gone, but America wanted to remember her and keep her memory alive.

MARGARET MITCHELL INFLUENCES THE LAW

Margaret Mitchell's influence was felt not only in literary circles but in the international legal world as well. When her novel was published, Margaret believed her United States copyright would protect her book all over the world. She was wrong.

At the time, the United States was not a member of the Universal Copyright Convention, so American authors were not protected in foreign countries. Margaret found that foreign publishers blatantly pirated *GWTW*. They changed the novel anyway they wanted, published the book without her permission, and refused to pay her royalties. The most brazen of these foreign pirates was a publisher in Holland, and Margaret fought for her rights in the Dutch court system.

On the home front, Margaret lobbied legislators and wrote to members of the State Department impressing upon them the need to extend United States copyright protection abroad. Unfortunately, Margaret's death ended her fight for America's authors. But her attorney brother, Stephens Mitchell, took up her battle in 1954 by presenting a summary of Margaret's *GWTW* copyright problems. This convinced Congress of the importance of international copyright protection, and the United States became a member of the Universal Copyright Convention the following year.

PROOF POSITIVE

Margaret left all rights to *GWTW* to her husband, John Marsh, who carried on the novel's daily business after her death. He also carried out his late wife's wish that her personal papers and manuscripts be destroyed.

But Marsh wanted to insure that Margaret's authorship of *GWTW* would never be questioned, so not all her papers were destroyed. He placed into a large envelope several typewritten chapters of *GWTW* with handwritten corrections, drafts of chapters with their changes, proof sheets, chronologies of the book's events compiled by Margaret, notes made by Margaret concerning the book, and several of the manila envelopes which had held Margaret's chapters during the writing of *GWTW*.

John sealed this large envelope, wrote his name over the seal, and placed the parcel in the care of the Citizens and Southern National Bank in July 1951. He also added a codicil to his will stating: "I am confident it can be proved not only that my wife, Margaret Mitchell Marsh, wrote *Gone with the Wind*, but that she alone could have written it." The package remains sealed to this day in the bank's vault.

John Marsh died on May 5, 1952. Under the terms of his will, the rights to *GWTW* were bequeathed to Margaret's brother, Stephens Mitchell, who oversaw the daily business of *GWTW* until his death in 1983.

FROM THE BIG SCREEN TO TV

HAPPY FIFTEENTH ANNIVERSARY, *GWTW!*

America couldn't wait for the fifteenth anniversary of *GWTW* in December 1954. So MGM decided to begin the celebration early with a May 20 anniversary "premiere" at the Loew's Grand Theatre in Atlanta.

Rich's department store joined in the festivities by featuring a display of Margaret Mitchell memorabilia. MGM and Atlanta's Smith College Club teamed up to host a "premiere" party. At the party it was announced that proceeds from premiere ticket sales would benefit the college's newly established Margaret Mitchell Scholarship. (Margaret's education at Smith had been cut short by her mother's death in 1919. But in 1939 the college granted Margaret an honorary master of arts degree.) There were more surprises the night of the premiere: *GWTW* had changed!

GWTW was now in CinemaScope. The film had been reprocessed for showing on the now-popular wide screen. The new process made the spectacular scenes more powerful, but the color was faded and grainy in certain parts of the film. MGM had made other alterations as well. *GWTW* had been transferred from volatile nitrate film to acetate safety film, thus preserving *GWTW* for the future. Another addition was Perspecta stereophonic sound.

From Atlanta, *GWTW* traveled to New York where it opened at Loew's State Theatre on May 29 and played for most of the summer. But the highlight of the fifteenth anniversary was the spectacular Hollywood premiere at the Egyptian Theatre on August 10.

Hollywood's top stars attended the glittering fete. On display in

151

the lobby were the Oscars *GWTW* had won, along with David O. Selznick's Thalberg Award. A touching ceremony honored the surviving stars of the film as well as its producer. Then the guests took their seats to view the "new" *GWTW*—still the greatest motion picture ever made.

ATLANTA REMEMBERS

The City of Atlanta chose the fifteenth anniversary of the film to honor the memory of the book's author. The Atlanta Council named a street Margaret Mitchell Drive. The Atlanta Board of Education christened a new elementary school the Margaret Mitchell School. In the auditorium, a portrait of Vivien Leigh as Scarlett O'Hara was unveiled. The Atlanta Public Library established the Margaret Mitchell Room as a site to exhibit a collection of Mitchell materials bequeathed by John Marsh.

HIGH-FIDELITY *GWTW*

In 1954, fans could not only see *GWTW* in theaters, they could listen to *GWTW*'s music on their hi-fi's. RCA Victor released a ten-inch, long-playing album of *GWTW* music written and conducted by Max Steiner. But this wasn't a soundtrack. Steiner composed a special arrangement of *GWTW*'s individual themes. The music was interpreted by a thirty-piece orchestra under Steiner's direction.

The best-known of *GWTW*'s themes, "Tara's Theme," also acquired a lyric by Mack David in 1954. Titled "My Own True Love," the song was a successful recording for several vocalists.

THE NOVEL GOES PAPERBACK

GWTW enjoyed its sixty-eighth printing in 1954. It retailed for $4.50 although a $2.95 cheap edition was also available. But in April, Margaret Mitchell's book made history again: It was published in paperback.

Doubleday, owner of the subsidiary rights, announced a Permabook edition of *GWTW*. The book, which the company called "the longest modern pocket-sized book ever to be published" had 864 pages and sold for 75 cents.

THE NOVEL:
TWENTY YEARS AND COUNTING

In June 1956, *GWTW* celebrated its twentieth anniversary of publication. Macmillan proudly announced that worldwide sales hovered at around eight million copies. Readers in twenty-five countries were enjoying editions of *GWTW* printed in twenty-seven different languages.

THE RECORD BREAKER'S
RECORDS ARE BROKEN

Until the 1950s, no other film had come close to breaking *GWTW*'s championship records for winning the most Academy Awards and being the top box-office grosser. But inevitably, the records were to fall.

In the Oscar category, 1953's *From Here to Eternity* and 1954's *On the Waterfront* both equaled *GWTW*'s sweep of eight Academy Awards The 1958 musical *Gigi* was victorious in every category for which it was nominated and captured nine Oscars. However, one of the categories was Best Costume Design—a category that did not exist in *GWTW*'s days—so Windies refused to concede the championship. The record was broken for good, though, with the 1959 appearance of MGM's *Ben-Hur*. This spectacular religious production earned a total of eleven Academy Awards exactly twenty years after *GWTW*'s own record-setting win.

GWTW's championship as top box-office grosser also fell in 1960. In *Variety*'s yearly list of the top ten money-making movies, Cecil B. DeMille's *The Ten Commandments* took control of the number-one position with total rentals of $34,200,000. *GWTW* had slipped to second place with a total of $33,500,000.

GWTW CELEBRATES
THE CIVIL WAR CENTENNIAL

In honor of the one-hundredth anniversary of the Civil War, MGM planned another Atlanta "premiere" of *GWTW* for March 10, 1961 which promised to duplicate the hoopla of the film's 1939 debut.

The Hollywood contingent, including Vivien Leigh, Olivia de

Havilland, and David O. Selznick, arrived at the airport and were greeted by welcoming crowds and brass bands. The celebrities then enjoyed a motorcade along Peachtree Street, which was lined with waving, enthusiastic fans. That evening, a Centennial Benefit Costume Ball was held at the Biltmore Hotel. Guests at the Ball included the governors from eleven Southern states.

The following evening, attendees entered the glittering Loew's Grand Theatre and took a step back in time. The theater was decorated exactly as it had been in 1939. But many things had changed since that time, and this premiere was bittersweet for the surviving members of GWTW's family. So many of those connected with the film were gone, including Clark Gable, who had died of a heart attack just four months before. When Gable appeared on the screen at the foot of the Twelve Oaks staircase, Vivien Leigh gasped, "Oh look at Clark; he looks so young and gorgeous!" However, the film's message of hope for tomorrow sliced through the momentary gloom. The thunderous applause that filled the theater at the end of the film acknowledged once again how much audiences loved GWTW.

After the Atlanta premiere, GWTW opened at the Hollywood Paramount Theatre in Los Angeles on March 24 and at the Loew's State Theatre on Broadway in New York City on April 26. The film played other first-run engagements in America and Canada then made the rounds of smaller neighborhood theaters.

Audiences may have noticed that the film's color was darker than they remembered. This was because of a new technique called Metrocolor that was used to process new prints of the film and that replaced the more expensive Technicolor process. Fans didn't care. GWTW was back, and they flocked to see it.

At the end of 1961, GWTW had earned another $7.7 million, which boosted it back to the top of Variety's list of champions with total rentals of $41,200,000. In second place was Ben-Hur ($40,000,000), and in third place was The Ten Commandments ($34,200,000).

POSTSCRIPT ON DAVID O. SELZNICK

The Academy Awards for GWTW sealed David O. Selznick's reputation as producer extraordinare. Yet in the years that followed, Selznick was haunted by the ghost of GWTW.

The specter loomed before him with every film he considered. If the new project would not be as great at GWTW, he turned it down. He bought the rights to The Keys of the Kingdom and Waterloo Bridge.

But when he could not get excited about making the films, he sold the rights to other studios. To keep his studio financially afloat, he loaned his stable of stars to other producers.

"You know what my problem is?" he said during a story conference. "I know that when I die the stories will read, 'David O. Selznick, producer of *Gone With the Wind*, died today.' I'm determined to leave them something else to write about."

Selznick thought he'd found that "something else" in a new actress discovered by Kay Brown and in a best-selling novel written by Margaret Buell Wilder.

Selznick found shy, retiring newcomer Phyllis Isley fascinating. He placed her under contract, began grooming her, and changed her name to Jennifer Jones. He initially matched her with Twentieth Century-Fox director Henry King, who was looking for an unknown to star in *The Song of Bernadette*. Jones landed the role, and her star was on the rise.

The novel, *Since You Went Away*, dealt with another war, World War II, and the changes it brought to the lives of an American family. Selznick thought this would be the perfect vehicle for Jones and bought the rights for $30,000.

Selznick was excited about filmmaking again. He wrote the script, chose the director, and selected the distinguished cast, which included Claudette Colbert, Shirley Temple, and Lionel Barrymore. During the filming, Selznick also fell in love with his leading lady. Selznick crowned the 1944 film with the slogan: "The four most important words since *Gone With the Wind—SINCE YOU WENT AWAY!*" The film was a success, but it wasn't a *GWTW*. Selznick, still feeling the need to better his best, began searching for another project.

The next film was *Duel in the Sun*, starring Jennifer Jones, Gregory Peck, and Joseph Cotten. Almost from the beginning the film was beset with problems, such as script rewrites, fights, firings, and reshootings. It took Selznick over two years and $6 million to complete the project. He viewed the 1946 film as a western version of *GWTW*. The critics hated it.

By this time Selznick was reeling from personal as well as professional crises. His marriage was over; his brother Myron was dead; and Selznick seemed to have lost his movie-making touch. The cost overruns for two films, *The Paradine Case* and *Portrait of Jennie*, had drained the company's finances. Selznick was $12 million in debt and had no other choice but to liquidate the company in 1949. Most of the studio's assets were sold, including the costumes used in *GWTW*, and Selznick withdrew from filmmaking to pay off his debts and to contemplate his future.

The hope of making another *GWTW* rekindled for Selznick in 1957 when he decided to remake *A Farewell to Arms*. As his stars, he chose his new wife Jennifer Jones and Rock Hudson; for the script, he tapped Ben Hecht. In a memo to Hecht, Selznick implored, "Let's really try to do a job that will be remembered as long as *Gone With the Wind*, something that we can be proud of in the years to come." The movie turned out to be quite the opposite. Critics blasted the film for its poor acting, overproduction, and antiquated style. Selznick was devastated, and *A Farewell to Arms* was his farewell to the movie industry.

In 1961, when MGM honored the Civil War Centenary by re-releasing *GWTW* and restaging the Atlanta premiere, Selznick was reunited with the two surviving stars of his epic: Vivien Leigh and Olivia de Havilland. He seemed lethargic and disinterested during the ceremonies that preceded the showing of the film. When he was introduced and came on stage, though, the wild applause of the crowd seemed to electrify him. The hard years peeled away from his lined face. He brushed back his white hair, stood tall, and basked in the adulation.

GWTW was now a benevolent spirit. If Selznick couldn't beat it, he would join forces with it. So Selznick decided to turn *GWTW* into the greatest musical Broadway had ever seen.

He needed to secure the stage rights and entered into negotiations with the agent who represented Margaret Mitchell's estate—Kay Brown, the former Selznick associate who had urged him to buy the film rights to the novel. Once the stage rights were his, Selznick began looking for the best composers and writers. Richard Rodgers and Oscar Hammerstein II turned him down, as did Harold Rome and Dimitri Tiomkin. They feared that their stage version would compare poorly to the film. Selznick planned to write the libretto himself and even thought about building a grand-scale theater specifically for the magnificent production he envisioned. But he was unable to unite the elements he needed to create the *GWTW* musical, and the idea died.

The man who produced *GWTW* died of a heart attack on June 22, 1965. He was 63. And newspaper obituaries across the country remembered Selznick just as he had always thought they would.

GWTW REACHES THE STAGE

David O. Selznick had dreamed of bringing *GWTW* to Broadway. He was not able to realize this dream in his lifetime, but he probably would have been pleased to know that *GWTW* finally made it to the off-

Broadway stage. Way off Broadway. In fact, the play *GWTW* debuted in Japan.

The five-hour production opened on November 3, 1966 at Tokyo's Imperial Theatre. Although the play had twenty-one scenes, it covered only the first half of the novel. Still, the production ran for five months, and in its 197 performances drew a total audience attendance of 380,000.

A second play with a running time of four hours opened the following summer and presented the second half of the novel. This play was as successful as the first and enjoyed four months of performances. Then in the fall of 1967 the two plays were combined, and a condensed six-hour version hit the stage.

GWTW IN 70mm SPLENDOR

Bigger isn't always better, and this axiom was proved true in 1967 when *GWTW* was reissued in a 70-millimeter wide-screen version. In the

PHOTO BY GEORGE

THE POSTER ISSUED WITH THE 70-MM
WIDE-SCREEN VERSION IN 1967

process, each of *GWTW*'s 35-millimeter frames was stretched to fit the wider 70-millimeter format. To achieve this, however, the tops of heads and the bottoms of legs were sacrificed, ruining the composition. The film's title lost its sweeping grandeur, too. The main title was replaced with four small words, stationary on the screen.

Another new feature was the addition of a stereophonic soundtrack, very different from the enhancement made in 1954. The new soundtrack amplified sounds such as the rustle of hoop skirts or the clop of horses' hooves, but often these extraneous sounds muffled essential dialogue.

Despite its drawbacks, this latest version of *GWTW* kept theater seats filled. At the close of 1967, *GWTW*'s total rentals reached $47,400,000. One year later, at the end of the first-run engagements, the total had soared to $70,400,000. Although *GWTW* had been on the top of *Variety*'s list of box-office winners for weeks, it was supplanted at the end of 1968 by *The Sound of Music*, whose higher-priced tickets brought rental totals to $72,000,000.

GWTW: ALL IS FORGIVEN

In 1968 the National Catholic Office for Motion Pictures had a change of heart about *GWTW*. The former Legion of Decency took another look at the film and reclassified *GWTW* as "morally unobjectionable for adults and adolescents."

Why the turnabout after nearly thirty years? In the words of the National Catholic Office, "the social changes following World War II have made what once appeared as daring scenes seem almost innocent on the screen today."

GWTW: THE MUSICAL

If *GWTW* could be transformed into a play, could a musical be far behind? A musical version of *GWTW* called *Scarlett* opened at Tokyo's Imperial Theatre on January 2, 1970.

Playwright Kazuo Kikuta wrote the script based on his 1966 stage version. Broadway veteran Harold Rome wrote the music and lyrics, and award-winning Broadway stager Joe Layton was director and choreographer. Toho Company, Ltd., a Japanese conglomerate, put up $1.7 million for the four-hour musical, which played to standing-room-only audiences.

After its Tokyo run, *Scarlett* was translated into English and headed to the British stage. The musical, under the creative direction of Joe Layton, opened on May 3, 1972 at London's Theatre Royal, Drury Lane. Show business writers called the production, with an estimated budget of $450,000, the most expensive musical ever staged in London.

Although audiences thrilled to the staged spectacle, including the nightly burning of the Atlanta depot, the critics were less impressed. Critic Haskel Frankel, writing for the *National Observer*, noted: "The biggest disappointment is American Harve Presnell as Rhett Butler. He has the looks and voice for the part, but God's gifts are all he brings to the role; Presnell doesn't even attempt the Southern accent, and he's about as dashing as warm water." Frankel was kinder to the leading lady. "The surprising star is June Ritchie as Scarlett. A British actress, she is as Southern as a julep and, if not as ruthless as she should be, Miss Ritchie at least manages to smoulder in the part."

Scarlett crossed the Atlantic and opened in Los Angeles on August 28, 1973. Lesley Ann Warren and Pernell Roberts took over the principal roles, but the critics gave the production many failing marks. On October 23, 1973 the musical debuted in San Francisco, again, to poor notices.

Sherry Mathis as Scarlett and David Canary as Rhett took a touring version of the musical on the road. The musical played to theater audiences in the South with stopovers in Dallas, Kansas City, Miami Beach, and Atlanta. However, the dream of making it to Broadway faded.

"THE ELEGANCE AND GLAMOUR OF HOLLYWOOD DESIGN"

In November 1974, New York's Metropolitan Museum of Art played host to an exhibit of more than one hundred Hollywood costumes. The lavish collection titled "The Elegance and Glamour of Hollywood Design" was assembled by that grande dame of fashion, Diana Vreeland.

Among the costumes displayed were Mae Murray's waltz gowns from *The Merry Widow*; Joan Crawford's red, bugle-beaded sheath from *The Bride Wore Red*; Audrey Hepburn's ascot dress from *My Fair Lady*; and Marilyn Monroe's pleated skirt from *The Seven Year Itch*, complete with sidewalk grating that blew hot air under the hem.

GWTW was represented as well. The displays included Scarlett's green-sprig muslin dress, her wedding gown, the green-velvet drapery dress, her New Orleans honeymoon dress, and Bonnie Butler's blue-velvet riding habit.

THE NOVEL'S
FORTIETH ANNIVERSARY

To celebrate *GWTW*'s anniversary in 1975, Macmillan published a slipcased anniversary edition of the novel. The special edition, which retailed for $14.95, contained an introduction written by James A. Michener.

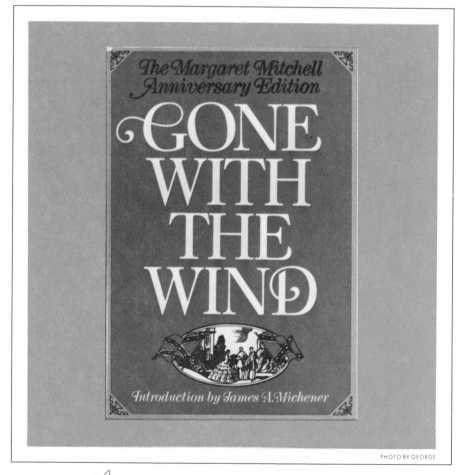

PHOTO BY GEORGE

THE FORTIETH ANNIVERSARY EDITION OF THE NOVEL, PUBLISHED IN 1976.

Macmillan also published two books with *GWTW* tie-ins. *Scarlett, Rhett and a Cast of Thousands* by Roland Flamini told the story of the making of the movie. *Margaret Mitchell's GONE WITH THE WIND Letters 1936–1949*, edited by Richard Harwell, was a collection of 333 letters showing how the publication of *GWTW* changed Margaret Mitchell's life.

ALL ABOARD!

In the bicentennial year of 1976, Americans from coast to coast boarded the American Freedom Train, a ten-car rail caravan that contained 750 historical mementos of America's past. For a small admission, visitors toured the Freedom Train on a moving walkway and saw such items as a copy of the Constitution owned by George Washington and the baseball and bat Hank Aaron used to break Babe Ruth's home run record.

The eighth car was dedicated to "The Performing Arts." Among the display items were Fred Astaire's top hat and the dress Judy Garland had worn in *The Wizard of Oz*. *GWTW* was represented as well. There among the artifacts were Clark Gable's leather-bound *GWTW* script and a brooch Vivien Leigh had worn as Scarlett.

GWTW'S WORLD TELEVISION PREMIERE

The National Broadcasting Company paid $5 million to MGM for the one-time showing of *GWTW*. Everyone was waiting for the classic film to appear for the first time on television. But as it turned out *GWTW* did not make its world television premiere on NBC.

While NBC was busy selling commercial time at a record $234,000 a minute, MGM struck a deal with Home Box Office. The deal allowed HBO to broadcast *GWTW* commercial free fourteen times during the month of June 1976. On June 11 at 2:30 P.M. *GWTW* made its actual world television premiere on cable—five months before its network debut.

Dick Cavett was the genial host for *GWTW*'s world premiere. He shared with the cable audience some of the stories connected with the casting and filming of Margaret Mitchell's masterpiece. The film was then shown in its uninterrupted entirety, and the broadcast was repeated that evening at 8:00. Twice-a-day broadcasts took place on six other dates in June, and cable viewers loved it. *Variety* later estimated that

382,500 viewers, which is more than 85 percent of HBO's total audience of 450,000 subscribers, had watched the film at least once.

GWTW ON NETWORK TELEVISION

In the midst of a presidential election that saw Georgia-born Jimmy Carter elected to the Oval Office, America's attention turned to another "native" of that fair state: Scarlett O'Hara. NBC would be broadcasting *GWTW* on two successive nights, November 7 and 8, 1976.

TV Guide featured Scarlett and Rhett on its cover that week, and in "This Week's Movies" section reviewer Judith Crist stated: "This is *Gone with the Wind*'s week, and television, via NBC will be on trial with its presentation of the 1939 classic." Crist expressed concern about the distribution of seventy-eight minutes of commercials and station breaks during the film. NBC also planned to extend Part One beyond the normal intermission break.

Olivia de Havilland had already expressed her displeasure about the manner in which the film would be broadcast. NBC had asked her to introduce the film, but she had refused. "I was appalled to learn that they planned to give so much time to commercials . . . a break in the showing every twenty minutes. I object to that," de Havilland said.

Despite her objections, on Sunday, November 7 at 8:00 P.M. the announcer for *The Big Event* called *GWTW* "the most eagerly awaited event in television history." Then, even before the film began, the network went immediately into commercials.

The film opened as usual with the Selznick International trademark and the running of credits. Then Scarlett was on the porch with the Tarletons and discovers that Ashley is to marry Melanie. The Sunday night presentation of *GWTW* continued past Scarlett's vow to never be hungry again, and the broadcast ended with Scarlett starting her lumber business with Ashley's help.

The conclusion of *GWTW* took place the next evening, Monday, November 8, ironically the anniversary of Margaret Mitchell's birth. But instead of being *The Big Event*, *GWTW* was billed as *Monday Night at the Movies*. The trademark and credits were run again, then NBC provided a synopsis of what had been shown the night before. Finally, viewers rejoined the story as Scarlett becomes a businesswoman and followed her (with commercials, of course) through to her tearful final scene.

GWTW AND THE NEILSEN RATINGS

How did *GWTW* fair in the ratings war? According to the Nielsen ratings, the Sunday, November 7 broadcast of the film had a 47.6 rating and a 65 percent audience share. The Monday, November 8 broadcast had a 47.4 rating and a 64 percent audience share. When the figures were combined and averaged, *GWTW* scored an overall rating of 47.5 and a 65 percent of total audience. In terms of actual numbers, NBC estimated that 33,890,000 homes had watched *GWTW* on Sunday and 33,750,000 on Monday. NBC proudly proclaimed that *GWTW* was "the highest-rated television program ever presented on a single network."

TELEVISION PARODIES OF GWTW

GWTW was in for some high-spirited ribbing after making its television debut. During a John Denver special, Joanne Woodward, in a Southern-belle organza gown and a straw picture hat, sat in a rowboat munching an apple and clutching a parasol. Courting beau Denver worked the oars as well as his charms. The placid scene was interrupted by the menacing music from *Jaws*, and then suddenly the great white himself rose up from the water. One gigantic gulp later, the ocean denizen had devoured Denver, half the boat, and had turned Scarlett O'Woodward into the Lady of the Lake.

Carol Burnett's parody of *GWTW* was a rollicking sketch called "Went With the Wind." Burnett as "Starlett O'Hara" tormented Dinah Shore's "Melody" until that gentle soul finally pushed "Starlett" down a staircase. Vicki Lawrence fared just as well. She played "Sissy," a white servant, who took great pleasure in returning a slap across the face to her domineering mistress. Harvey Korman was a dashing "Rat Butler" in the funniest portion of the sketch. He greeted "Starlett" as she walked down the staircase of her plantation home in her drapery dress, drapery rods still in place.

AT LONG LAST, THE SEQUEL

◆

THE CONTINUATION OF *GWTW*

After *GWTW* was published, fans inundated Margaret Mitchell with mail asking what happened after Rhett walked out on Scarlett. Margaret was always firm: "I do not have a notion of what happened to them and I left them to their ultimate fate. With two such determined characters, it would be hard to predict what would happen to them." She rejected both Selznick's and MGM's requests to write a sequel, and after her death in 1949, her brother Stephens Mitchell continued refusing sequel offers through the 1950s and 1960s.

But Stephens was aware that the battle could not be waged forever. He was getting on in years and couldn't remain Margaret's champion indefinitely. Also, the expiration of *GWTW*'s copyright in 2011 would no doubt unleash countless continuations of the story. So in the 1970s, Stephens began to consider authorizing a sequel.

In 1975, Kay Brown, the agent for Margaret's estate, met with Richard Zanuck and David Brown of Universal, who were famous for producing grand-scale movies such as *Jaws* and *The Sting*. Would they be interested in a sequel to *GWTW*? They jumped at the chance. MGM claimed some rights to a sequel, however. An option deal was worked out that brought Universal and MGM into partnership for a sequel to *GWTW*.

Zanuck and Brown estimated that their budget for *Gone With the Wind, Part II* would be jointly financed by Universal and MGM to the tune of about $12,000,000. They also stated that in their casting of the leading roles they would not seek out performers who looked like Clark Gable or Vivien Leigh.

The writer selected for the screenplay was Anne Edwards, author of *Judy Garland* and a soon-to-be-published biography of Vivien Leigh. But instead of a screenplay, Edwards offered to write a book instead. The book could be adapted into a screenplay, and the book's paperback publication could be timed to coincide with the release of the film.

The 775-page book that Edwards submitted, *Tara, The Continuation of Gone with the Wind*, supposedly was set in 1872–82 and showed a divorce for Scarlett and Rhett, a subsequent remarriage for Scarlett, and more intrigue between the former Mrs. Butler and her ex. Although producers Zanuck and Brown were satisfied with the project, MGM was not. MGM turned thumbs down on Edwards's book and the screenplay written by James Goldman. The book was shelved, and the deal collapsed.

THE CBS DEAL FOR *GWTW*

In April 1978, CBS and MGM concluded an unprecedented twenty-year deal for *GWTW*. CBS bought exclusive television rights to broadcast the film twenty times during the length of the agreement at a price tag of $35 million, the largest license fee ever paid for a single film in the history of television.

GWTW COLLECTOR PLATES

In 1978 the Edwin M. Knowles China Company, under the aegis of Metro-Goldwyn-Mayer, introduced the official *GWTW* commemorative plate collection. The beautiful *GWTW* series was painted by artist Raymond Kursár.

"Scarlett," the first issue in the series, originally sold for $21.50. But the limited-edition, hand-numbered plate proved so popular with both Windies and plate collectors that its value has skyrocketed to nearly $300. The plate depicted Scarlett, with billowing organdy skirts in hand, dashing through azaleas and dogwood with Tara in the background.

The second plate in the series was "Ashley." The artist portrayed a uniformed Ashley descending the Twelve Oaks staircase as he is about to ride away to war. However, the reserved, aristocratic Mr. Wilkes wasn't

PHOTOS BY GEORGE

GWTW COLLECTOR PLATES FROM THE EDWIN KNOWLES CHINA COMPANY.

a hit with collectors, who bypassed this quintessential Southern gentleman in favor of the third plate, "Melanie," and the fourth plate, "Rhett." "Melanie" showed the gentle Mrs. Wilkes waiting outside Aunt Pittypat's house for Ashley's return. "Rhett" pictured Mr. Butler, outspoken and independent, against the extravagantly decorated library in Scarlett's Atlanta house.

Suddenly collectors decided "Ashley" was the one for them after all. Collectors scrambled to complete their series but found that the price for "Ashley" in the secondary markets soared as high as $225.

In 1988, as a follow-up to the first series, MGM and Turner Entertainment Company authorized the *GWTW* Golden Anniversary Plate series. This limited-edition, hand-numbered plate series was painted by artist Howard Rogers and carried the hallmark of W.S. George Fine China.

The first issue, "Scarlett and Her Suitors," showed a flirtatious Scarlett surrounded by beaux at the Twelve Oaks barbecue. The original issue price was $24.50, and the plate was limited to 150 firing days.

STEPHENS MITCHELL GOES TO COURT

In 1981 Stephens Mitchell took MGM to court to challenge the studio's assertion that it held certain sequel rights. MGM stated that Stephens had relinquished sequel rights when MGM's option on his sister's novel was renegotiated in 1961.

The court battle raged for four years and ended in fall of 1985 with the Eleventh District United States Court of Appeals ruling in favor of Margaret Mitchell's estate. Stephens Mitchell died in 1983, and his two sons, Eugene Muse Mitchell and Joseph Reynolds Mitchell, are now Margaret's heirs.

Before his death, Stephens Mitchell entrusted the *GWTW* fight to three Atlanta lawyers. They have so far prevented a civic group from performing a parody of *GWTW* and refused to allow a California seed company from naming a new tomato the Scarlett O'Hara. Stephens also placed in their hands the responsibility for arranging a sequel to *GWTW*.

GWTW ON VIDEOCASSETTE

"If you could own just one film on videocassette," the ad read, "which would it be? Of course it would." The *GWTW* video that Windies had hungered for hit the market in March 1985. The double-cassette deluxe edition carried a price tag of $89.95.

The production of the video was as meticulous as Selznick's production of the film itself. MGM/UA Home Video gave the nod for the project to Crest Labs in Hollywood, a house known for its high-quality work. In executing the transfer from film to tape, Crest Labs labored scene by scene, making restoration repairs to the visual frames and to the soundtrack. The result is a *GWTW* that looks and sounds better than ever.

As soon as the *GWTW* video appeared on store shelves, it soared toward the top of the sales chart. For a solid three weeks it was the number-two best seller behind *Star Trek III*. Almost half a million *GWTW* videocassettes were sold by 1987 alone. Only time will tell if *GWTW*, in VHS or Beta, goes on to make video sales history.

MACMILLAN CELEBRATES *GWTW*'S FIFTIETH BIRTHDAY

In 1986, to mark the half-century birthday of its best-selling book, Macmillan published 60,000 copies of a special *GWTW* anniversary edition. The golden anniversary edition was a facsimile of the first edition right down to a faithful reproduction of the original book-jacket artwork. The facsimile's prepublication price was set at $9.95; the price after June 30 was $16.95.

And fans of the novel rushed to buy copies. In fact, sales were so great that *GWTW* climbed back on the best-seller list again, just in time for its birthday.

Stamped into History

Even the United States Postal Service joined in the celebration of *GWTW*'s fiftieth anniversary. On June 30, 1986 the Postal Service issued a one-cent Great American stamp bearing the likeness of Margaret Mitchell. The stamp's artist, Ron Adair of Richardson, Texas, based his design on a photograph of the author.

The stamp was unveiled at a first-day issue ceremony held at Atlanta's Omni International. Butterfly McQueen attended the event and was presented with an album of the new stamps. Following the festivities, Windies and stamp collectors alike besieged a nearby postal booth and cleaned out the stock of 50,000 Margaret Mitchell stamps.

PHOTO BY GEORGE

THE MARGARET MITCHELL POSTAGE STAMP ISSUED IN 1986.

Other Golden Anniversary Celebrations

• The residents of Clark Gable's home town, Cadiz, Ohio, kicked off *GWTW*'s golden anniversary year by honoring The King of Hollywood on the eighty-fifth anniversary of his birth. A seven-foot granite and bronze monument was dedicated to Gable on February 1, 1986 and placed at the site of his birth on Charleston Street.

• Collier Books, Macmillan's paperback division, reprinted *Margaret Mitchell's GONE WITH THE WIND Letters, 1936–1949.*

• Dell re-released *Road To Tara: The Life of Margaret Mitchell* by Anne Edwards.

• Avon enlivened its *GWTW* paperback with a new anniversary cover.

• Outlet Books released *David O. Selznick's GONE WITH THE WIND* by Ronald Haver.

• Book-of-the-Month Club offered a deluxe anniversary edition of *GWTW* with an introduction written by Tom Wicker.

• The Madison-Morgan Cultural Center in Madison, Georgia offered an exhibit from April 4 to May 25, 1986 called "The Big Book: Fifty Years of *Gone with the Wind*." The exhibit featured American and foreign editions of the novel, photographs and stills from the movie, and letters written by Margaret Mitchell.

• A Norwegian magazine sponsored a *GWTW* Trivia Contest with the first prize of a trip to Jonesboro, Georgia going to Finn and Lilleba Galaas of Norway.

• Macmillan sponsored a raffle at the New Orleans convention of the American Booksellers Association. The prize was a first edition of *GWTW*.

• The Franklin Mint offered a Scarlett O'Hara porcelain doll for $195 and for $500 a coral replica of the necklace Scarlett wore at the Twelve Oaks barbecue.

• The Canfield Casino in Saratoga Springs, New York was the place to be on August 1, 1986 as Mr. and Mrs. Cornelius Vanderbilt Whitney (Sonny and Marylou to their friends) threw a *Gone With the Wind* Party. (Whitney and his cousin John "Jock" Whitney had financed Selznick International.) Famous for her annual theme parties for the thoroughbred set, Mrs. Whitney arrived in a horse-drawn landau. She wore a replica of the green-sprig muslin dress, complete with picture hat that Scarlett wore to the Twelve Oaks barbecue. The *GWTW* theme was continued in the menu with barbecued chicken and ribs, steakburgers, and a salad bar.

GWTW COLLECTOR EXTRAORDINARE

When it comes to *GWTW* memorabilia, a retired postman from Sharpsburg, Georgia believes he has the world's largest collection.

Herb Bridges, who headed Atlanta's Fiftieth Anniversary Celebration, estimates that his collection includes thousands of items such as photos, movie posters, lobby cards, dolls, foreign and domestic editions of the book, and other *GWTW* mementos.

LIBRARY PATRONS LOVE *GWTW*

The poll wasn't scientific; it was just for fun. But the majority of patrons polled at local libraries voted *Gone with the Wind* "the best book read," according to the American Library Association (ALA). The informal survey of 62,200 readers was conducted in April 1987 in conjunction with National Library Week.

TED TURNER ACQUIRES MGM LIBRARY

Turner Broadcasting System, Inc., bought the MGM library of films, including *GWTW*, almost lock, stock, and barrel in 1986. Not part of the deal, though, were the television rights to *GWTW* that CBS had acquired from MGM in 1976.

In 1987, however, the Atlanta-based Turner Broadcasting System announced that a deal had been struck with CBS for the television rights. Specific terms of the arrangement were not released, but part of the negotiations gave CBS additional broadcasts of another 1939 MGM classic, *The Wizard of Oz.*

AT LAST, THE SEQUEL TO *GWTW*

Will Scarlett and Rhett get back together? The question that Windies have been asking for the last fifty years is about to be answered. In 1987, the committee of three Atlanta attorneys representing Margaret Mitchell's estate gave the go-ahead for an authorized sequel.

Working with the William Morris Agency, the committee considered twelve candidates for the project before finally selecting novelist Alexandra Braid Ripley, a native of Charleston, South Carolina. According to Robert Gottlieb, Ripley's agent, she has "the skill and sensibility to bring the post-Civil War era—and the formidable Scarlett—back to life."

The plot of the sequel will be developed by Ripley in consultation with the committee, since the lawyers want to make sure that the integrity of Margaret's novel remains intact. Although Ripley plans to handle sex more openly in her novel, she will avoid graphic sexuality. She also plans to avoid the thick slave dialect favored by Margaret. Ripley believes it is difficult to read and demeaning to blacks.

The Morris Agency circulated among publishers an outline of the sequel and two sample chapters written by Ripley in advance of the novel's auction held in April 1988. Of the six publishing houses that participated in the spirited bidding, Warner Books came out on top with a bid of $4.94 million. The novel is expected to debut in hard cover in 1990 and in paperback in 1991 in the United States and Canada. And the price for the expected 1000-page hardcover book? Probably around $25. Ripley's novel will be the basis for the subsequent motion picture or television miniseries.

Alexandra Braid Ripley must pick up where Margaret Mitchell left off, and Ripley is up to the challenge. She is the best-selling author of "big, fat, serious historicals" such as *Charleston, On Leaving Charleston, New Orleans Legacy,* and *The Time Returns.*

Ripley is well connected to the world of Scarlett and Rhett. She grew up in Charleston, South Carolina, the soul of the South and Rhett Butler's home town. As a child, she took nickels from tourists in return for directions to Rhett Butler's grave.

She attended Ashley Hall, a Charleston finishing school, where she learned deportment by walking up stairs balancing a book on her head. "Because of Charleston's isolation and clannishness, I was fifty years out-of-date," Ripley says. "I feel as if I grew up in Margaret Mitchell's generation."

A scholarship from the United Daughters of the Confederacy allowed her to attend Vassar College. After graduation, she joined *Life* magazine's advertising department in New York. She held a series of other jobs north of the Mason-Dixon line and married and divorced before returning to Charleston with her daughters Elizabeth and Merrill. Ripley settled in a house that had once been a home to slaves and began a career as a ghostwriter.

She returned to New York a few years later and accepted a job as a reader of unsolicited manuscripts at a publishing house. By the time she became publicity director, she decided to try writing her own books. A mystery novel followed, then a joint venture involving a nonfiction account of a murder and a ghosted autobiography. By that time, her money was running low.

A 1975 visit to Virginia convinced Ripley that the modest standard of living there would allow her to write *and* to eat. So she moved south again and found a job as a bookstore stock clerk. In 1981 *Charleston* was published. Customers flocked to the bookstore to buy the book and to have the novel autographed by the author right in the stockroom. *Charleston,* set in the post–Civil War era, received outstanding reviews from critics who compared the book with *GWTW.* Ripley's career was launched.

Today Ripley and her second husband John Graham, a professor of rhetoric, call home an eighteenth-century country farmhouse in central Virginia. To prepare for writing the sequel to *GWTW,* Ripley read Margaret's novel at least six times, looking for dates and studying the language. She hand-copied two hundred pages of the book to experience Margaret's style. "My hand just won't write 'fiddle-dee-dee,' she told *Life* magazine. "But I figure in my 1,000-page book I'll have to give them at least three and throw in 'God's nightgown!' 'Great balls of fire!' and 'As God is my witness!' "

As part of her research, Ripley made several trips to Atlanta and Charleston. She studied train timetables between those two cities from the year 1873, maps of city streets, letters, diaries, and old newspapers. Scenes from the movie helped her imagine the rooms in Scarlett's Atlanta house. Ripley chose Charleston buildings dating from the sequel's period as Rhett's town house and the home of Scarlett's aunts.

Like Margaret Mitchell, Ripley gives the cold shoulder to being a celebrity. In fact, she says, "I'm trying to prepare myself for a universal hatred of what I'm going to do." She also acknowledges that the sequel "will never be mine. It's a foster mother kind of thing."

But the sequel and the money she earns from it will allow her to do what she loves to do: write. Future projects include a book about a tobacco baron, one on Joseph of Arimathea, and one on Marquis de Lafayette. But the project that Windies are anxiously awaiting is the sequel to *GWTW*. Just what adventures does Ripley have in store for Scarlett and Rhett? We can hardly wait to find out!

SEQUEL NOTES

• Although it took Margaret Mitchell ten years to write *GWTW*, Ripley has eighteen months to deliver her manuscript.

• *Life* magazine will publish an excerpt of the sequel just before the novel is published in 1990.

• Just to break even on its investment, Warner Books needs to sell about 250,000 hardcover and three million paperback copies of the sequel.

• How the sequel ends will be the best kept secret in publishing. President of Warner Books, Laurence Kirshbaum, quips, "We're going to hire the security guards from Fort Knox to watch over the ending."

• A publishing house in France has paid $1 million for the rights to publish the French version of the sequel.

GWTW IS CAUGHT IN THE WAR
BETWEEN THE COUNTIES

The war in Georgia raged for over a year. The dispute? Which county, Clayton or Coweta, would build a *GWTW* theme park.

Clayton County, south of Atlanta, believes it has the literary rights to *GWTW*. After all, both Margaret Mitchell in her novel and David O. Selznick in his film set Tara smack-dab in Clayton County. In spring 1986 county officials announced that a memorial to Margaret Mitchell and her novel would be built just as soon as the millions of dollars needed for the project could be raised. The nonprofit project would include an exhibition center with a small theater and life-size replicas of Tara and the Atlanta train station. The site of the project would be land once owned by Margaret Mitchell's great-aunts, Mary and Sarah Fitzgerald.

Nearby Coweta County, on the other hand, has plenty of money ($20 million raised by private investors) plus something extra: the facade of Tara from the movie set. Betty Talmadge, former wife of former Georgia Governor and U.S. Senator Herman E. Talmadge, bought the facade many years ago and recently agreed to sell the structure to Dunaway Gardens Restoration Inc., which plans to build the theme park.

The Coweta County project would include a working plantation complete with the restored Tara façade, an amphitheater, a wildlife preserve, and the renovated Fitzgerald homestead, which was moved from its original site in Clayton County. As a child, Margaret visited the Jonesboro farmhouse with her family and was entertained with stories about the Civil War.

The two sides exchanged increasingly heated volleys in the ongoing war of words between the counties. Then in October 1987, the Clayton County project was knocked out of the running. Clayton County voters rejected a $23 million plan to finance the *GWTW* attraction with an increase in sales tax revenue.

That leaves only the Coweta County theme park, and Betty Talmadge feels it will finally be built. "When people go out West they want to see cowboys," she says. "When they come to Atlanta they want to see Scarlett and Rhett."

DON'T DUMP "THE DUMP"

The Atlanta apartment where Margaret Mitchell gave birth to Scarlett O'Hara may soon be gone with the wind unless a preservation group is successful in its efforts to save "The Dump."

After their marriage in 1925, Margaret Mitchell and John Marsh were in debt because of John's recent medical bills. Since they were on a tight budget, they set up housekeeping at the Windsor House, a three-story, Victorian-style apartment building on Crescent Avenue. Their ground-floor apartment offered two shabby rooms plus a kitchen and bath, so Margaret promptly nicknamed their accommodations "The Dump."

Margaret was confined to The Dump in 1926 because of a sprained ankle, and there she began writing her novel. She set up her mother's old sewing table in the living room in a windowed alcove decorated with panels of beveled mirrors. Pounding away on a Remington portable, she completed all but three chapters of *GWTW* during the seven years she lived on Crescent Avenue.

Since Margaret's days, the Windsor House has seen even harder times. Students, hippies, and vagrants called it home at various times through the years, and today it stands boarded up and abandoned.

But The Dump stands on a prime piece of real estate, just off Atlanta's famous Peachtree Street. The owner of the property, Trammell Crow Company, a Dallas real estate developer, is seeking to demolish the house to put up a building complex, while the nonprofit Mitchell House Inc. is seeking $1 million in funding to restore the site. The two sides continue to clash, and this fight may prove even hotter than Sherman's march to the sea.

GWTW GLASNOST

During the fourth Reagan-Gorbachev Superpower Summit in 1988, the press center in Moscow featured a display of a dozen books by American authors. The books were translated into Russian and the languages of other Soviet republics. Among the selections was Margaret Mitchell's epic with a slightly askew translation title: *Carried Out With the Wind.*

SCARLETT, CONTROL THAT BALL GOWN

Would-be Scarletts will no doubt receive a good number of invitations to *GWTW*-dress parties honoring the fiftieth anniversary of the film. The question is, How do you fit a hoop skirt into a Plymouth Horizon?

Actually, antebellum-style gowns are quite smooshable. So it is possible to dress like a Southern belle and still remain a lady.

Sitting in a crinoline gown is perhaps the number-one problem. Do it incorrectly and you'll look like a giant bell, and no Southern lady wants her legs confused with a clapper. So just before you sit down, pick up the back of the hoop. Keep the hoop in the middle of your back and arrange the fullness of the skirt around you.

Moving around in a *GWTW* ball gown can be equally as tricky. When walking, take small steps and maintain good posture. Otherwise, the hoop will sway.

When you want to go through a doorway, push the sides of the dress in. The same rule applies when you are entering a car. When exiting the car, just hold the gown down around you.

Why fiddle-dee-dee, it's as easy as can be! And no Rhett Butler will be able to resist you!

LOOK WHAT THEY'VE SAID

◆

MEMORABLE QUOTES ABOUT *GWTW*

"Forget it, Louis. No Civil War picture ever made a nickel."

During a conference with Louis B. Mayer, MGM's production chief Irving Thalberg listened to a story synopsis of an about-to-be-published Civil War novel. Thalberg's comment prompted the studio head to turn down movie rights to *GWTW*.

"I beg, urge, coax, and plead with you to read this at once. I know that after you read the book you will drop everything and buy it."

Katherine (Kay) Brown, story editor of Selznick International Pictures's New York office, was excited after reading *GWTW*, which had been submitted to her by agent Annie Laurie Williams. Along with the novel and a synopsis, Brown sent to Selznick this enthusiastic message.

"Scarlett is going to be a difficult and thankless role. The one I'd like to play is Rhett Butler."

After her fans reacted negatively to rumors of her playing Scarlett, Norma Shearer explained to *The New York Times* why she withdrew from contention for the role.

"Oh, you don't want to be in *Gone With the Wind*, it's going to be the biggest bust in town."

> Jack Warner tried to dissuade Olivia de Havilland when she expressed an interest in playing Melanie.

"I guess we're stuck with you."

> At a Hollywood party, George Cukor's comment to Vivien Leigh was her first hint that she had captured the role of Scarlett O'Hara.

"Yesterday I put on my Confederate uniform for the first time and looked like a fairy doorman at the Beverly Wiltshire—a fine thing at my age."

> A disgruntled Leslie Howard shared his feelings about playing Ashley in a letter to his family.

"At noon I think it's divine; at midnight I think it's lousy. Sometimes I think it's the greatest picture ever made. But if it's only a great picture, I'll still be satisfied."

> David O. Selznick commented on the film to reporters the night before *GWTW*'s Hollywood press preview.

"No movie has a right to be that long!"

> Franklin Delano Roosevelt fell asleep during a screening of *GWTW* at the White House and awoke with very critical comments about the film.

"Oh dear, do you realize that poor Melanie will not be in it?"

> Olivia de Havilland's reaction upon hearing that producers Richard Zanuck and David Brown were planning a sequel to *GWTW*.

"I'm quite sure that Clark Gable, Vivien Leigh, and Leslie Howard are up there somewhere right now incensed over the proceedings."

> Olivia de Havilland was angered that *GWTW's* network television premiere would be marred by numerous commercial interruptions.

"My favorite scene was the burning of Schenectady, New York and President Grant surrendering to Robert E. Lee."

> Jimmy Carter's joke caused peals of laughter in the audience at the American Film Institute's gala honoring *GWTW* as the greatest American film.

"This is terrific. We now have the television rights to the greatest movie ever made."

> Ted Turner was thrilled after Turner Broadcasting System, Inc. bought from CBS all the television rights to *GWTW*.

"Yes, Margaret Mitchell writes better than I do—but she's dead."

> Alexandra Braid Ripley acknowledged she has a tough act to follow in writing the sequel to *GWTW*.

"We wanted to be the first to know what happened to Rhett and Scarlett."

> Laurence J. Kirshbaum, president of Warner Books, quipped about his company's $4.94 million bid for the right to publish the sequel to *GWTW*.

Answers

GWTW: A NOVEL QUIZ, pages 9-11

1. He had killed an English absentee landlord's rent agent.

2. James and Andrew O'Hara

3. In poker games

4. Pork

5. Mammy

6. Robillard

7. Philippe Robillard

8. In a barroom brawl in New Orleans

9. Sixteen

10. Katie

11. Lemon verbena

12. Fayetteville Female Academy

13. Susan Elinor and Caroline Irene

14. Three. They died in infancy.

15. Frank Kennedy

16. Brent Tarleton

17. To buy Pork's wife, Dilcey, from John Wilkes.

18. Prissy

19. Honey and India Wilkes

20. Charles Hamilton favored Honey; Stuart Tarleton courted India.

21. Beatrice

22. A horse breeding farm

23. They all had red hair.

24. Tom, Boyd, and twins Stuart and Brent

25. Jeems

26. After his wife's death, he married his children's Yankee governess.

27. After the death of her fiance, Cathleen Calvert married her family's Yankee overseer.

28. Wade Hampton Hamilton, Ella Lorena Kennedy, Bonnie Blue Butler.

29. Atlanta received its name the same year Scarlett was born.
30. Sarah Jane Hamilton
31. Uncle Peter
32. Henry Hamilton
33. Five hundred dollars
34. K.
35. Rhett Butler
36. Rock Island, Illinois
37. John Wilkes
38. September 1
39. A radish
40. Mimosa
41. In the diaper of Melanie's son
42. The kitchen
43. Will Benteen
44. Suellen O'Hara
45. He was accused of having killed a black.
46. Tony Fontaine
47. Carreen entered a convent.
48. Archie
49. Mr. Butler
50. Twenty-eight

THE MOVIE MOGULS SELZNICK BESTED WITH HIS *GWTW* BUY, page 18

1. e
2. f
3. d
4. a
5. c
6. b

THE GREATEST MOVIE OF ALL TIME, pages 97-99

1. Brent and Stuart Tarleton
2. Ashley Wilkes was engaged to marry his cousin, Melanie Hamilton.
3. To tell Ashley she loved him so he wouldn't marry Melanie
4. Which gown to wear to the barbecue
5. Cathleen Calvert
6. West Point
7. A vase / Rhett Butler
8. Charles Hamilton (Melanie's brother)
9. Pneumonia following an attack of measles
10. $150 in gold
11. Aunt Pittypat

12. A hat
13. Three days
14. Major
15. Scarlett promised to look after Melanie.
16. $50 in gold wrapped in Rhett Butler's handkerchief
17. Above the Red Horse Saloon
18. Dr. Meade / Melanie was in labor.
19. Prissy
20. Ashley's picture and Charles's sword
21. He wanted to join the Confederate army.
22. Ellen O'Hara (Scarlett's mother)
23. That she will never be hungry again
24. A Yankee deserter
25. $300
26. Jonas Wilkerson
27. Emmy Slattery
28. From Ellen O'Hara's draperies
29. Rhett Butler
30. The condition of her hands
31. Frank Kennedy / Her sister, Suellen

32. At the counter of the Wilkes and Kennedy store
33. The lumber business
34. Shantytown / Big Sam
35. Melanie, Scarlett, Mammy, India Wilkes, and Mrs. Meade
36. *David Copperfield*
37. Ashley
38. He proposed marriage.
39. A red taffeta petticoat
40. Twenty inches
41. India Wilkes and Mrs. Meade
42. Ashley's birthday party
43. London
44. Bonnie missed her mother. She was terrorized by nightmares in the dark.
45. Scarlett fell down the staircase at her Atlanta home.
46. Bonnie had just learned to ride sidesaddle.
47. Melanie
48. A mateless glove
49. Charleston
50. Scarlett decided to return to Tara and to think of a way to get Rhett back.

THE PLAYERS WHO'S WHO, page 102

1. h
2. e

12. f
13. s

3. p	14. l
4. i	15. b
5. n	16. j
6. a	17. g
7. m	18. t
8. q	19. v
9. r	20. k
10. c	21. d
11. o	22. u

WHO SAID IT? (#1), pages 102-105

1. Rhett (in the library at Twelve Oaks after Scarlett smashed the vase against the mantle)

2. Scarlett (stirring a kettle of soap and greeting Pork returning from town where he had learned that the taxes on Tara were going up)

3. Ashley (during the scene of Melanie's death)

4. Rhett (as he was about to walk out on Scarlett)

5. Melanie (after Scarlett's shooting of the Yankee deserter)

6. Rhett (in his buggy after rescuing Scarlett from the fleeing crowds in the Atlanta streets)

7. Ashley (as he said goodbye to Scarlett at the end of his Christmas leave)

8. Rhett (warning Scarlett what would happen if she didn't have Bonnie's things packed for the trip to London)

9. Melanie (after giving Ashley the tunic she had made for him as a Christmas present)

10. Scarlett (after telling Frank Kennedy that Suellen was engaged to marry one of the County boys)

11. Ashley (after Scarlett's declaration of love in the library at Twelve Oaks)

12. Rhett (as he left Scarlett at Melanie's front door on the night of Ashley's birthday party)

13. Ashley (following Scarlett's declaration of love in the library at Twelve Oaks)

14. Scarlett (speaking to a drunken Rhett in their Atlanta diningroom

following Ashley's birthday party)

15. Rhett (after presenting the Paris hat to Scarlett)

16. Scarlett to Ashley (during the scene of Melanie's death)

17. Scarlett (after she was attacked at Shantytown)

18. Ashley (during the discussion of the possibility of war as the gentlemen enjoyed brandy and cigars at Twelve Oaks)

19. Rhett (speaking to Mammy after Bonnie's birth)

20. Rhett (during the escape from Atlanta)

21. Scarlett (her plea to Mammy who caught her trying on a colorful bonnet while in mourning for Charles)

22. Melanie (meeting Scarlett at Twelve Oaks)

23. Rhett (while dancing with Scarlett at the Atlanta Bazaar)

24. Ashley (speaking to Melanie during the barbecue at Twelve Oaks)

25. Rhett (as he walked out on Scarlett)

26. Scarlett (speaking to Rhett before she drove to the lumber mill via Shantytown)

27. Rhett (speaking to his card-playing Yankee captor in the Atlanta jail)

28. Scarlett (speaking to Ashley in the lumber mill office on the afternoon of his birthday)

29. Melanie (speaking to Mammy following Bonnie's birth)

30. Ashley (after Scarlett's declaration of love in the library at Twelve Oaks)

31. Scarlett (following Rhett's walking out on her)

32. Melanie (when Melanie thanks Belle Watling for saving Ashley's life)

33. Rhett (speaking to Scarlett on the road to Tara before leaving her to join the army)

34. Scarlett (on Tara's front porch with Brent and Stuart Tarleton)

35. Rhett (following Prissy's pleas outside Belle's establishment for Rhett to bring his carriage for Scarlett)

36. Scarlett (following her declaration of love to Ashley in the library at Twelve Oaks)

37. Scarlett (after Rhett bid for her to lead the opening reel at the Atlanta Bazaar)

38. Rhett (at Twelve Oaks with the gentlemen enjoying brandy and cigars)

39. Scarlett (after her declaration of love to Ashley in the library at Twelve Oaks)

40. Scarlett (during various episodes of her life)
41. Rhett (during the discussion of the possibility of war as the gentlemen
were enjoying brandy and cigars at Twelve Oaks)
42. Scarlett (in her bedroom at Tara following Charles's death)

THE MASTER'S *GWTW* GAME: MINOR CHARACTERS MATCH, page 105

1. e	7. g
2. i	8. a
3. b	9. j
4. f	10. l
5. h	11. d
6. k	12. c

WHO SAID IT? (#2), pages 106-107

1. Gerald O'Hara (speaking to Scarlett in the fields of Tara on his return from a visit to Twelve Oaks)
2. Suellen O'Hara (during nap time after the barbecue)
3. Charles Hamilton (during the discussion of the possibility of war as the gentlemen were enjoying brandy and cigars at Twelve Oaks)
4. Gerald O'Hara (speaking to Scarlett in the fields of Tara on his return from a visit to Twelve Oaks)
5. Suellen O'Hara (reacting to Scarlett's marriage to Rhett Butler)
6. Ellen O'Hara (comforting Scarlett, who has objected to wearing black mourning garments)
7. India (pleading to Doctor Meade about Melanie, who is on her death bed)
8. Cathleen Calvert (speaking to Scarlett on the staircase of Twelve Oaks on the day of the barbecue)
9. Frank Kennedy (following Scarlett's outburst at the mill to stop bothering her and not to call her Sugar.)

10. India Wilkes (speaking to Scarlett during the evening sewing circle)

11. Gerald O'Hara (speaking to Scarlett following her return to Tara)

12. India Wilkes (during the evening sewing circle)

13. Carreen O'Hara (picking cotton with Suellen in Tara's field)

14. Frank Kennedy (asking Scarlett for Suellen's hand in marriage)

15. Charles Hamilton (comforting his weeping bride on their wedding day)

16. Frank Kennedy (to Scarlett following her tour of his Atlanta store and lumber mill and her invitation for dinner and a visit)

17. Carreen O'Hara (speaking to Suellen, who reacted badly to Scarlett's plans to restore Tara and to build a house in Atlanta)

WHO SAID IT? (#3), pages 107-108

1. Uncle Peter (chasing Belle Watling from the steps of the Atlanta hospital)

2. Beau Wilkes (during the scene of Melanie's death)

3. Dr. Meade (speaking to Aunt Pittypat, who has questioned the propriety of Scarlett and Melanie remaining in Atlanta unchaperoned)

4. Bonnie Butler (speaking to Rhett before her fatal pony ride)

5. Uncle Peter (stalking the rooster that would become Christmas dinner in honor of Ashley's holiday homecoming)

6. Aunt Pittypat Hamilton (at the Atlanta Bazaar)

7. Bonnie Butler (her exclamation of delight as Rhett announced he will take her on a trip to London)

8. Mrs. Meade (questioning Dr. Meade as he searched for a probe with which to treat Ashley's wound)

9. Beau Wilkes (during the scene of Melanie's death)

10. Mrs. Merriwether (speaking to Mrs. Meade of Rhett's love for his daughter, Bonnie.)

11. Aunt Pittypat Hamilton (before fleeing Sherman's cannon balls that were raining on Atlanta)

WHO SAID IT? (#4),
pages 110-111

1. Jonas Wilkerson (the evening Mrs. O'Hara returned home from the bedside of Emmy Slattery)

2. Mammy (announcing to Scarlett the arrival of Rhett Butler after Frank Kennedy's funeral)

3. Belle Watling (referring to Scarlett, when Melanie thanks Belle for saving Ashley's life)

4. Mammy (holding back Scarlett as Ashley returned home from the war)

5. Belle Watling (outside the Atlanta hospital)

6. Mammy (after Scarlett sees Belle Watling going to visit Rhett in the Atlanta jail)

7. Yankee major playing cards with Rhett in the Atlanta jail.

8. Mammy (after Scarlett refused to eat before going to the barbecue)

9. Prissy (during Melanie's labor)

10. Yankee deserter to Scarlett at Tara

11. Mammy (after Mrs. O'Hara decided to send Scarlett to Atlanta to visit Melanie and Aunt Pittypat)

12. Mammy (putting Frank Kennedy's pants into the boiling pot)

13. Belle Watling (when Melanie thanked Belle for saving Ashley's life)

14. Prissy (during Melanie's labor)

15. Pork (following Scarlett's return to Tara)

16. Jonas Wilkerson (while visiting Tara with his wife, Emmy Slattery Wilkerson)

17. Johnnie Gallegher (showing off the prisoners who will work in the lumber mill)

18. Scarlett's attacker at Shantytown

19. Big Sam (while rescuing Scarlett from her attack at Shantytown)

20. Tom, a Yankee captain (interrupting the evening sewing circle)

Bibliography

The author wishes to thank the following sources, which were invaluable during the writing of *The Complete GONE WITH THE WIND Trivia Book.*

Books

Behlmer, Rudy, ed. *Memo from: David O. Selznick.* New York: Viking Press, 1972.

Edwards, Anne. *Road to Tara.* New Haven and New York: Ticknor and Fields, 1983.

———. *Vivien Leigh: A Biography.* New York: Simon and Schuster, 1977.

Farr, Finis. *Margaret Mitchell of Atlanta: The Author of GONE WITH THE WIND.* New York: William Morrow & Company, 1965.

Flamini, Roland. *Scarlett, Rhett and A Cast of Thousands.* New York: Macmillan Publishing Co., Inc., 1975.

Gardner, Gerald and Harriet Modell Gardner. *Pictorial History of GONE WITH THE WIND.* New York: Bonanza Books, 1983.

Harris, Warren G. *Gable and Lombard.* New York: Simon and Schuster, 1974.

Harwell, Richard, ed. *Margaret Mitchell's GONE WITH THE WIND Letters 1936–1949.* New York: Macmillan Publishing Co., Inc., 1976.

Haver, Ronald. *David O. Selznick's GONE WITH THE WIND.* New York: Bonanza Books, 1986.

Hecht, Ben. *A Child of the Century.* New York: Simon and Schuster, Inc., 1954.

Higham, Charles. *Sisters: The Story of Olivia de Havilland and Joan Fontaine.* New York: Coward-McCann, Inc., 1984.

Howard, Leslie Ruth. *A Quite Remarkable Father.* New York: Harcourt, Brace and Company, 1959.

Howard, Ronald. *In Search of My Father.* New York: St. Martin's Press, 1981.

Katz, Ephraim. *The Film Encyclopedia.* New York: Thomas Y. Crowell, Publishers, 1979.

Lambert, Gavin. *GWTW: The Making of GONE WITH THE WIND.* Boston: Little, Brown and Company, 1973.

———. *On Cukor.* New York: G.P. Putnam's Sons, 1972.

Levy, Emanuel. *And The Winner Is—The History and Politics of the Oscar Awards.* New York: The Ungar Publishing Company, 1987.

Mitchell, Margaret. *Gone with the Wind.* New York: Macmillan Publishing Co., Inc., 1936.

Pratt, William. *Scarlett Fever: The Ultimate Pictorial Treasury of GONE WITH THE WIND.* New York: Macmillan Publishing Co., Inc., 1977.

Ragan, David. *Who's Who in Hollywood 1900-1976.* New Rochelle, NY: Arlington House Publishers, 1976.

Steinberg, Cobbett. *Film Facts.* New York: Facts on File, Inc., 1980.

Thomas, Bob. *Selznick.* New York: Doubleday and Company, Inc., 1950.

Tornabene, Lyn. *Long Live the King: A Biography of Clark Gable.* New York: G.P. Putnam's Sons, 1976.

Truitt, Evelyn Mack. *Who Was Who on Screen.* New York and London: R.R. Bowker, Co., 1983.

Walker, Alexander. *The Life of Vivien Leigh.* New York: Weidenfeld & Nicolson, 1987.

Wiley, Mason and Damien Bona. *Inside Oscar.* New York: Ballantine Books, 1986.

Newspapers and Magazines

American Film	*Newsweek*
Atlanta *Constitution*	*Parade*
Chicago Tribune	*People Weekly*
Cosmopolitan	*Poughkeepsie Journal*
Knickerbocker News	*Publishers Weekly*
Life	*Time*
Los Angeles Times	*Times Record*
The National Observer	*Times Union*
New York Daily News	*TV Guide*
The New York Times	*U.S.A. Today*
The New York Times Book Review	*The Wall Street Journal*

Index

THE COMPLETE GONE WITH THE WIND TRIVIA BOOK

Never the Twain Shall Meet, 41
New York Metropolitan Museum of Art, 159
New York premiere, 119-120
Newcom, James E., 72, 122
A Night at the Opera, 80
Ninotchka, 121, 122
No Man of Her Own, 23
No Time for Comedy, 37, 71
No, No, Nanette, 46, 141
Noel, Hattie, 43
North and South, Book II, 139
Northwest Passage, 145
Nothing Sacred, 67, 73, 140
Notorious, 67
Novel: critics' reactions (1936), 12-13; editions, 11-12, 147, 152, 160-161, **160**, 169; foreign editions, 146-147, 149, 174, 176; in time capsule (1938), 17; paperback, 152; sales, 1, 11-12, 147, 153; title source, 6 *See also* Mitchell, Margaret
Nugent, Frank, 120
The Nun's Story, 140
Nye, Ben, 72
Nye, Carroll (Frank Kennedy), 47, 102, 143

O

O'Hara, Carreen. *See* Rutherford, Ann
O'Hara, Ellen. *See* O'Neil, Barbara
O'Hara, Gerald. *See* Mitchell, Thomas
O'Hara, Scarlett. *See* Leigh, Vivien
O'Hara, Suellen. *See* Keyes, Evelyn
O'Neil, Barbara (Ellen O'Hara), 42-43, 82, 102, 140
Oberon, Merle, 54
Of Human Bondage, 38, 41
Of Human Hearts, 141
Of Mice and Men, 121
The Old Maid, 144
Oliver, Edna May, 122
Olivier, Laurence, 51, 53, 54, 55, 56, 71, 76, 114, **119**, 122, 127, 137-138
On Golden Pond, 144
On the Waterfront, 126, 153
Orchestra Wives, 141
Oscars. *See* Academy Awards
Our Town, 140

Ouspenskaya, Maria, 122
The Outlaw, 140
Outward Bound, 40, 41
The Oxbow Incident, 145

P

The Painted Desert, 23
Papillon, 144
The Paradine Case, 155
Paramount Pictures, 17, 18, 30, 80, 138, 139
Parker, Eleanor, 136
Parnell, 21
Parodies of *GWTW,* 132, 163
Parsons, Louella, 27, 29, 33-34, 85, 86
Peck, Gregory, 155
Peg O' My Heart, 40
The Petrified Forest, 38, 41
Peyton Place, 145
Photoplay, 19-20, 125
Pimpernel Smith, 135
Pinocchio, 146
Pioneer Pictures, 17
Pittypat, Aunt. *See* Aunt Pittypat
Plates, Collector, 166-168, **167**
Platt, Joseph B., 72
Plunkett, Walter, 72, 73-75
Pocketful of Miracles, 73, 140
Polk, Oscar (Pork), 132
Pomerory's Past, 45
Portrait of a Lady, 140
Portrait of Jennie, 155
Pranks on the set, 83
Premieres. *See* Movie premieres
Presnell, Harve, 159
Price, Waterhouse and Company, 121
Price, Will, 69
Pride and Prejudice, 141
Princess O'Rourke, 143
Prinz, Eddie, 72
Prissy. *See* McQueen, Butterfly
The Prowler, 141
Pulitzer Prize, 15, 49
Pygmalion, 38, 41

Q

Quality Street, 29
Quizzes, 9-11, 97-99, 102-108, 110-111; answers, 183-190

R

Raffles, 49, 138
The Rains Came, 124

Rains, Claude, 122
Raintree County, 73
Rathbone, Basil, 19
RCA Victor, 152
Reagan, Ronald, 176
Reap the Wild Wind, 132
Rebecca, 125
Red Dust, 65
Reeves, George (Stuart Tarleton), 47, 102, 144
Reid, Mrs. Ogden, 34
Reid, Wallace, 80
Reilly, Tommy, 132
Reinhardt, Max, 38
Rennahan, Ray, 72, 122
Reynolds, Marjorie (Guest at Twelve Oaks), 146
Rhett, Alicia (India Wilkes), 36, 102
Ripley, Alexandra Braid, 172-174, 181
Ritchie, June, 159
Ritter, Thelma, 136
Rivers, Gov. Eurith D., 114, 116
RKO, 18, 28, 30, 36, 73, 93
Roberts, Leona, 105
Roberts, Pernell, 159
Robin Hood, 36
Robinson, Edward G., 37, 41, 46
Rockefeller, Nelson, 117
Rodgers and Hammerstein, 156
Roemheld, Heinz, 94
Rogers, Hazel, 72
Rogers, Howard, 168
The Roman Spring of Mrs. Stone, 138
Rome, Harold, 156, 158
Romeo and Juliet, 41
Rooney, Mickey, 43, 122, 132
Roosevelt, Eleanor, 43
Roosevelt, Franklin D., 17, 180
Roots: The Next Generation, 139
Rose of the Rancho, 145
Russell, Jane, 136
Russian translation, 176
Ruth, Babe, 161
Rutherford, Ann (Carreen O'Hara), **42**, 43, 74, 102, 141

S

Saratoga, 44, 146
Sarasota Springs, New York, 171
The Scarlet Pimpernel, 41
Scarlett O'Hara's Younger Sister, 141